The Hedgehog's Dilemma

The Hedgehog's Dilemma

A Tale of Obsession, Nostalgia, and the World's Most Charming Mammal

HUGH WARWICK

B L O O M S B U R Y

NEW YORK   BERLIN   LONDON

Published by Bloomsbury USA, New York

All papers used by Bloomsbury USA are natural, recyclable products
made from wood grown in well-managed forests. The manufacturing
processes conform to the environmental regulations of the country of origin.

LIBRARY OF CONGRESS CATALOGING-IN-PUBLICATION DATA HAS BEEN APPLIED FOR.

ISBN-10: 1-59691-477-7
ISBN-13: 978-1-59691-477-3

First U.S. Edition 2008

1 3 5 7 9 10 8 6 4 2

Typeset by Palimpsest Book Production Limited, Grangemouth, Stirlingshire
Printed in the United States of America by Quebecor World Fairfield

To Tristan and Matilda and their wonderful mother,
my wife, Zoë

Contents

Acknowledgements

This book would not have been possible without the work of Pat Morris and Nigel Reeve. Their research, and the accessible way in which it has been presented, have opened up the world of hedgehogs to thousands of people.

Helen Conford had far more faith in me than I did and welcomed me into the fold at Penguin, steering the process of writing. And the rest of the team – wow – we have had a lot of good cake. Thank you.

Dave Shephard's illustrations have constantly made me smile.

Poppy Toland was the perfect guide and interpreter for my visit to China. And in America, Zug Standing Bear and Virginia Lynch opened their beautiful home and introduced me to the amazing world of hedgehog-pet-keeping. Thanks also to the International Hedgehog Association and the Hedgehog Welfare Society for inviting me, and to Kari Espelien, Donnasue Graesser and all their members who made for such a memorable experience.

Thanks to Fay Vass, at the British Hedgehog Preservation Society, who put up with an awful lot of random and urgent requests; and also to my fellow trustees, who help keep the society in fine fettle.

Throughout Britain there are hundreds of hedgehog carers, many of whom have helped. In particular, I must thank those who have allowed me to nose around their hedgehogs: Louise Brockbank, Dru Burdon, Janis Dean, Elaine Drewrey, Caroline Gould, Sue Kidger, Barbara Roberts and Les Stocker. Special mention must go to Gay and Andy Christie at Hessilhead for helping to save over a thousand Uist hedgehogs, on top of everything else they do.

I have tolerant friends who have heard me talk about this book for years. In the end it was Paul Kingsnorth, along with his wife, Nav Chhina, who helped create the breakthrough by introducing me to his – now our – agent, Patrick Walsh, who gave me the confidence to present the book to the wider world.

The strength of friendship has been vital – not just the support that I have received, but also the fact that so many of my friends have already written wonderful books. So, to Jay Griffiths, Mark Lynas, George Marshall and George Monbiot, I thank you for showing me it is possible.

Many other friends have helped hold my hand through the inevitable stresses of writing a book, in particular Theo and Shannon of the world's greatest band, Seize the Day, and Debbie and Graeme in Chester's Rainforest. Anne, Edward and Simon, thank you for your love and support. I realize that this list is probably dreadfully incomplete, so let me just say that these are some of the people who have made this project possible: Olaf Bayer, Elise Benjamin, Gillie Bonner, Jenny Broughton, Roz Kidman Cox, Nansy Eimhjellen, Christophe

Fraiser, Sandy Kennedy, Caroline Lowes, Gordon Maclellan, Ross Minett, Maria Parker, Els Payne, Phil Pritchard, Kerry Seel, Ulli Seewald, Craig Simmons, Ricarda Steinbrecher, Oliver and Lisbet Tickell, Rowan Tilley, Douglas and Melissa Walker, Lyn Wells, Kevin Woodbridge, Derek Yalden and Jin Yufang.

My family have put up with a lot. I have foisted most of the childcare on to my wife, Zoë. I owe her so much. And Mati and Pip, despite all the sleep you have stolen from me, the look of love and excitement on your faces as you discover the world around you is more than enough to see me through the hardest times.

My parents' love and support have always been so very important. They read and commented on earlier incarnations of most of the chapters, which gave me a real sense of whether I was making any sense. But my father died before the book was finished. I wish he hadn't. I hope that this would have made him proud.

Introduction

The evening had started, as they all do, with 'Jerusalem'. My talk had roamed across England's green and pleasant land, all the way up to the furthest Scottish islands. The audience had been expecting a lecture about the biology, ecology and physiology of hedgehogs. What they got was what my audiences always get, stories. The best lecturers I have had have not lectured, they have told stories that have stayed with me, and that is what I try and do whenever I get to talk to my favourite audience, the Women's Institute.

I had talked for an hour, including a moderate barrage of questions, and was about to sink my teeth into a slice of superbly moist coffee and walnut cake when the questions began again. During the talk they had all been quite practical: why are we seeing fewer hedgehogs; how can we make our gardens more hedgehog-friendly; aren't they all covered in fleas; and how do they mate? But as usual, when I joined the good women of Islip for tea and cake, the balance shifted. The questions moved from the practical to the more personal: how long have I been involved with hedgehogs; what got me started and – perhaps the most frequently posed – why?

Over the years of talking to groups like the WI it has been

these questions that have encouraged my absorption into the hedgehog world. Trained as an ecologist, I was already innately interested in the workings of hedgehogs. But what these opportunities allowed was for me to begin to question my own motives.

Why was I interested in hedgehogs? Well, to be honest it started out over twenty years ago in a very pragmatic way – an opportunity to do something interesting as a project for my degree. But as I got to spend more time in the company of hedgehogs, I became drawn further into their world – a poorly investigated world at that. There were basic aspects of hedgehog ecology to be uncovered, but that was not all; there was also an attendant peculiarity to observe. Not just in the undeniable cuteness of the little animal, but in the eccentricities that attach themselves to those most fond of them. Because the world of hedgehogs is inextricably tied up with the world of people. Not just in greetings cards and children's stories, but deeper – politics, passion and obsession.

Politics. Wildlife management is a fraught business – unpalatable decisions often have to be taken that result in animals being killed. And so it was with the Uists. The most outer of the Outer Hebrides, these islands became home to the biggest ever hedgehog story: the great battle of hedgehogs vs. birds, or at least their eggs – the very same collision that got me started on hedgehogs as a student. Needless to say, I became involved and was delighted to be partly responsible for ending the cull.

Passion. I have met many people who have dedicated themselves to looking after sick and injured hedgehogs. All over the country there are little hedgehog hospitals doing an amazing job with limited resources. While there are wildlife hospitals that take in a range of animals, hedgehogs are special in the attention they receive, partly due to their amenable nature, but mainly because of the love they inspire. And while it might seem odd to think of this as a reciprocal relationship, I did meet people who got as much out of the hedgehogs as the hedgehogs got from them.

Obsession. There are, however, people who take the relationship just a little further – some might argue that they take it just too far – and those are the hedgehog pet keepers of the USA. The strangeness of that world was wonderful to enter, and while I thought I was a little above it all, I was informed that I fitted right in . . . though I am not sure I fitted in with the talking hedgehog ghosts and the International Hedgehog Olympic Games.

My own passion has slipped a little over into obsession, or so I was told by my wife when I described my plans to head off to China to find a hedgehog called Hugh that had only been recorded twelve times in the last hundred years.

This book is as much about our relationship with hedgehogs as it is about hedgehogs themselves. There are more detailed treatises on the ecology, behaviour and physiology of the animal. Here I take the time to investigate what it is that hedgehogs mean to us, to try and answer the question of why they hold such a special place in our hearts.

There is no other wild animal that can compare to the hedgehog – no other animal that allows us to get as close.

Nose-to-nose with a hedgehog, you get a chance to look into its eyes and glimpse a spark of truly wild life.

At this point I lose some of my audience . . . but I will persevere. This connection with a wild animal is, I believe, a vital one. It allows us to appreciate the hedgehog in a way that we can with no other creature – and I would argue that it is the moment that we begin to fall in love with the natural world, moving out of a sentimental affection for it and into something deeper. And from there it is just a short step to wanting to do something about the parlous state we are in – hence the reason why I argue that hedgehogs can save the world.

And this is what is so great about the WI. I can talk about such existential ideas to an interested crowd of people and get to eat some of the finest cake known to humanity. It is no joke, the quality of WI cakes. So good are they that when I am asked about money for my talks I always give them the option of offering me a cake to cover my travel expenses . . . and it has to be coffee and walnut.

PART ONE

Them and Us

CHAPTER
ONE

*First of All,
What Is a
Hedgehog?*

Is this a ridiculous question? After all, surely everyone knows what a hedgehog is – there is no mistaking the small, brown, spiny mammal for anything else, unless, maybe, you are drunk and get it confused with a porcupine. Which is not a relative, by the way. Not at all. Porcupines are rodents, like rats and squirrels; hedgehogs are insectivores, related to moles and shrews.

And it is very unlikely that any of us are going to stumble upon a tenrec as we trundle around the garden, unless we have relocated to Madagascar and are very lucky, as they are quite rare. The spines on a tenrec do not denote a close kinship either; they illustrate the wonders of 'convergent evolution', where different animals end up with similar characteristics, despite springing from different roots.

Still, I feel the need to get a few of the basic facts down. I was with my daughter, Matilda, at a playgroup recently and was rather surprised to discover that one of the people I was talking to so lacked the basic knowledge of the hierarchies of life that she thought birds were mammals (I was talking about the strangeness that is the egg-laying mammals, such as echidnas and duck-billed platypuses).

That got me thinking. Why should I assume that people will understand where hedgehogs fit in in the great scheme of life? After all, I don't speak a second language, something which many people find absurd (including me).

So here are some basic facts about hedgehogs. Hedgehogs are placental mammals, which means that they have fur, give birth to live young and feed them with milk from mammary glands. Mammals are vertebrates, like birds, reptiles, amphibians and fish. Going in the other direction, hedgehogs belong to the group of mammals known as insectivores. These are the earliest of mammals and there are hedgehog-like fossils around from the last days of the dinosaurs.

The 'mother hedgehog' is thought to have emerged from Asia during the Eocene period, though there are fragments of hedgehog ancestors dating back to 70 million years ago – before the catastrophic end of the dinosaurs.

Our hedgehog in Britain, the western European hedgehog, like all species that have come to the attention of taxonomists, has a binomial name in Latin: *Erinaceus europaeus*. The word *erinaceus*, which comes from the Latin for hedgehog, represents the genus, while *europaeus* clearly refers to Europe and defines the species.

Taxonomy is wonderful. It allows us to see relationships between the myriad life forms with which we share this planet. It allows us to begin to make sense of the mind-boggling complexity of life. The binomial system was developed in the mid-eighteenth century by Carl Linnaeus. He was doing his best to reveal the genius of his God in the wonders of nature, but what his system has done is reveal the wonder of nature in itself.

We all know what a hedgehog looks like, but not everyone has managed to get as close to them as I have, so let's start with the most obvious – the spines. The back and sides of the hedgehog are covered in spines that are around 25 millimetres long and there are between 5,000 and 7,000 of them on an adult hedgehog. One of the many questions I am asked concerns babies, or more particularly how pregnant hedgehogs cope with the process of delivery. And a very good question that is too, as baby hedgehogs are born with spines. But their skin is inflated with fluid, keeping the prickles beneath the surface. After birth, the fluid is absorbed and the spikes emerge.

The spines are, in fact, just modified hair. And in our, western European, hedgehog these are usually banded, dark at the base, followed by a light band, another dark band and culminating in a light tip. I say 'usually' with regards to the coloration because there is quite a lot of variation, as seen particularly with the island population on North Ronaldsay, Orkney, as well as those on the Channel Island of Alderney. Then there are the occasional albinos, white all over with a pink nose and eyes.

Whatever the colour, the spines are absent from the face, throat, chest, belly and legs. These are covered in fur, usually grey/brown and fairly coarse, though quite strokeable when compared with the spines. But then again, when a hedgehog is in the right mood, even the spines are pleasant to stroke – a bit like pushing your hand into a bag of Puy lentils (I recommend you try: each lentil is hard but the overall effect is comforting and smooth). It is only when the hedgehog becomes displeased that the small muscles at the base of each spine are sent a message, causing the spines to erect. We all have that capacity, to a rather lesser extent. The hairs on our arms will erect when exposed to cold air.

The defensive strategy of the hedgehog does not rest alone with the spines; there is also the ball. This is a near-perfect defence, unless, of course, the threat is a badger with long claws, or a car. Rolling into a ball is something we can just about imagine. The muscle that allows the balling is the frown muscle – *panniculus carnosus*. Go on, frown. Feel the way that the forehead is pulled down? Now imagine that the muscle wrinkling your forehead actually stretches all the way to your coccyx and, as you frown, all the spines across your back get pulled to attention.

But you will have to do it faster than that. If you ever try to take a photograph of a hedgehog you will notice a twitch that is the beginning of the great frown. I have so many pictures of hedgehogs that include a small blur where the face should be. Within 0.01 seconds of the noise of the camera being operated, the forehead muscle contracts, the head jerks down and the tiny muscles at the root of each spine are stimulated, causing the hedgehog to bristle. So set a very fast shutter speed.

Back as a hedgehog, bring your nose to your tail and retreat into a ball, using the convenient skirt of skin that hangs almost to the ground. This skirt is bounded by an amazing muscle, the *orbicularis*, which acts like a drawstring, pulling the hedgehog-ball shut.

This skirt is something that taxidermists seem to fail to understand with depressing regularity. When presented with a spiny corpse, they simply stuff it, giving no thought to the hedgehog's skirt, so the stuffed hedgehog ends up looking like a prickly football. Just because the skin is there does not mean it needs stuffing.

In some hedgehogs the skin does get well and truly stuffed. In the news recently there was a hedgehog found that weighed in at a massive 2.2 kilos (it had apparently been eating the bread left out for the birds and looked as if its legs were not going to be able to reach the ground). Usually our hedgehogs range in size from 450 grams up to around 1.2 kilos. They tend to be about 20–30 centimetres long.

The skirt of skin – which provides the excess to envelop the balled-up hog – hides four legs of surprising length, up to 10 centimetres from hip to toe. The usual image of the hedgehog is of the clockwork toy – or one of the people from Trumpton, rolling about on invisible wheels. But there are four legs busy at work. I suppose a hedgehog is a little like a swan – serenely floating across a lake, but with webbed feet working hard below the surface. It is only when the hedgehog wants to move with speed that it hoicks up its skirt of skin, revealing the elegant legs, and off it goes.

Or up it goes. They can climb with some agility, if no great sense. I met a man who described watching a hedgehog in his garden determinedly walking in a straight line. When confronted by the wire container of grass cuttings, rather than take the very short detour around, it began to climb the vertical structure. On reaching the top, over a metre up, it toppled into the clippings, padded its way across to the other side, clambered up again before tumbling to the ground and continuing on its way, unflustered by the experience. While that reveals great things about hedgehogs' ability to climb, it does not say much for their intelligence.

The climbing gets them into some rather unlikely corners. I received a letter from Elizabeth Hibbert in Walthamstow, Greater London, indicating a hedgehog's great determination to scale the heights. She was disturbed in the dead of night, in her first-floor bedroom, by an animal. At first she thought it a large rat, but then found it to be a hedgehog, which promptly scurried away under a large wardrobe. Where it stayed for several days, until a man from a wildlife rescue centre came and helped extricate the animal. Whether this rescuer should be allowed out in public, though, is another matter: he claimed to have seen a hedgehog running across the North Circular Road at night, standing on its hind legs.

One of the reasons why hedgehogs are so adept at climbing is that they possess highly effective shock absorbers: their spines. Where the prickle emerges from the skin it is a little thinner and slightly angled. This bends and cushions the fall of a careless hedgehog and also has the advantage of preventing the spines from being driven back into its body.

Their ability to survive a tumble does not make them careless of gravity, though, which is fortunate, as gravity presents the best way of unrolling a reluctant hedgehog. Unrolling a hedgehog is not gratuitous; it is the only way of telling boys from girls.

First, pick up your hedgehog. I tend to use lightweight gardening gloves, but if you are careful and blessed with rhino skin, you can get away without. I am assuming the hedgehog will be in a ball – they usually are (you would be too if a monster was to tower some 20 metres above your head). Go gently: always gently, these are precious creatures to be treated with great respect.

So, to unroll, place the bundle of spines in both hands. Have a close look and see where the nose meets the tail; have the nose side of the ball on one hand and the tail on the other. Gently raise one hand and then the other, rocking the animal by only a couple of centimetres. Gradually start to shift the hands apart and, usually, the hedgehog prefers to unravel rather than tumble.

Now, if you just want to take a peek and check the sex, lift the front up. If it has a penis it is male. The penis is the bit that looks rather like a tummy button, about 3–5 centimetres in front of the tail. So as long as you can get them to unroll, that should be straightforward. Apart from when they are quite young, as then the unrolling is much harder. Sometimes the umbilical cord can cause confusion too in new-born animals.

But if you are lucky enough to have a reasonably compliant hog in your hands, why not have a closer look at the amazing body? It might let you stroke its tummy – some do – though be aware that the balling mechanism is fast and can leave you wearing a pretty painful glove, fingers trapped inside.

While you are there, check out the legs. They are as long as they are because they have more to deal with than just locomotion. They allow the hedgehog to groom. I have had people tell me that the reason hedgehogs are notoriously riddled with fleas is that the spines prevent them from grooming properly, but a hedgehog can reach around with its rear feet, feet that support considerable claws, and have a good scratch.

Most hedgehogs have five toes on their feet, apart from the four-toed hedgehog, that is, which has – well, I am sure you don't need help – four toes, but only on its rear feet. And we must not forget the tail – there is nearly 2 centimetres of tail.

With all those spines, you have to ask yourself, why are hedgehogs nocturnal? Why go to all that bother to protect yourself if you are just going to hide away in the shadows? Well, for mammals, our behaviour is the odd one – being diurnal is peculiar. And as for the hedgehog, it is simple: while the spines lend protection, they are not perfect, and, most importantly, hedgehog food is nocturnal. All those mini-beasts prefer the damper, cooler nights, away from the birds and the desiccating sun.

It is easy to look at hedgehogs on their nightly patrols, stumbling through the undergrowth, and think that they have poor eyesight. Well, as one writer has pointed out, if we had our noses just a few centimetres off the ground among the mud and grass, we would not be able to see much. In fact, hedgehogs' eyes are pretty sharp and they may have some limited colour vision. But the main cues they rely on are sound and smell.

Just listening to a hedgehog in the undergrowth makes it clear how important smell is – all that snuffling is not an indication of a cold and neither is their perpetually wet nose. The moisture assists the uptake of scent. As for sound, well, hedgehogs have quite selective hearing – like my children, I suspect. They are much better at hearing high-frequency noises – if you jangle keys near a hedgehog you will get a very swift response. They cannot rely on sound too much, though, given the racket they can make when moving through the undergrowth.

I received a letter from Julian Greenwood, who, when a young army officer out on exercises with his unit one night, discovered just how much noise they can make. While planning an attack he heard a sound which he took to be an enemy patrol. Swiftly he established an ambush, but even with night-vision equipment they were unable to spot the intruder, who was getting closer. Really admiring the camouflage, they readied weapons, issued a challenge and then Julian started laughing as the inquisitive hedgehog meandered through his legs.

While it is dangerous to generalize, these basic physiological traits are probably fairly consistent across the range of hedgehogs. We must remember that we are not the only people with hedgehogs in the world. There are twenty different species, though I feel I should take some issue with the point at which a hedgehog becomes a hedgehog. Surely spines should be a defining feature. Starting with the spiny ones, the most authoritative list of hedgehog species was set out by fellow hedgehog expert Nigel Reeve. He lists them as:

Erinaceus europaeus ('our' hedgehog)
Erinaceus concolor (eastern European hedgehog)
Erinaceus amurensis (Russia, China, Korea)
Paraechinus aethiopicus (Ethiopian hedgehog, found from Morocco to Arabian peninsula – it has long ears)
Paraechinus hypomelas (Brandt's or long-spined hedgehog – from Iran and Afghanistan to Pakistan)
Paraechinus micropus (pale or Indian hedgehog)
Atelerix albiventris (central African or white-bellied hedgehog)
Atelerix algirus (Algerian hedgehog – also found in coastal regions of southern France)
Atelerix frontalis (southern African hedgehog)
Atelerix sclateri (Somalian hedgehog – which may be related to white-bellied)
Hemiechinus auritus (long-eared hedgehog – found from Ukraine to China, with subspecies along the way)
Hemiechinus collaris (Hardwicke's or collared hedgehog – eastern Pakistan and north-western India)

 Hemiechinus dauricus (China)
Hemiechinus hughi (China)

Others disagree and have found another couple of species, and then there is the business of hairy hedgehogs. This might come as a shock – and a disagreeable one at that – but there are some hedgehogs that do not have spines. When is a hedgehog not a hedgehog? When it is a gymnure or moonrat, found in high forests of South-East Asia. While lacking the defensive attributes of spines, these hairy hedgehogs do have pronounced anal glands, and the greater moonrat is reckoned to smell of garlic, sweat and rotten onions. Nice.

In the UK we are at the western edge of the hedgehog's range. They stretch all the way across to China and down to South Africa. They are found in deserts and woodland, but not up mountains or deep in bogs.

They used to live in America, in the wild. But that was a long, long time ago. I was in touch with a palaeontologist, Tom Rich, who wrote his PhD thesis on these prehistoric hogs. Studying fossils from an extinct genus of hedgehog, *Brachyerix*, that roamed the earth between 5 and 20 million years ago, in the Miocene, he was able to show that while hedgehogs have not undergone the sort of dramatic evolutionary change of, say, horses and whales, they are not unchanged from the earlier models. I love the idea that Miocene literally translates as 'less recent'. Over 20 million years ago certainly strikes me as less recent. But then that is putting a very human perspective on it all. The planet has been here for over 4,000 million years, so, relatively speaking, the Miocene is not that far off at all.

But far enough to save us from confronting one of the Miocene hedgehogs, *Deinogalerix*, which translates as 'terrible shrew' (Shakespeare would have had fun taming this one). This animal, remains of which were found in modern-day Italy, was over three times the size of our hedgehog and, while lacking spines, did have some rather disturbing teeth.

Anyway, there are no hedgehogs living in the wild in the Americas, unless some of the pet pygmy hedgehogs, introduced from Africa, have escaped and set up camp.

With the sort of arrogance that comes from a colonial past, some have named the African hedgehogs pygmy hedgehogs. Yes, the species from Africa are all smaller than the European ones; in fact, all the species of hedgehog are smaller than the European ones, so perhaps it would be fairer to call the European hedgehogs 'giant', as opposed to labelling all the others 'pygmy'.

Labelling hedgehogs is a fun thing to do – and I have been searching for different names the hedgehog has been given, over the years and around the world. But where did 'hedgehog' come from? Was it because of their habit of hogging hedges? I have heard from people who declare that the 'hog' is because they taste like pig, or that it is the distinctive snuffling that generated the name. Then one day I saw a photograph of a spineless specimen – not a quivering wimp of a hog, but one with no prickles. And in that shape I could see a wild boar. A very small wild boar, but there all the same.

The following is more a sample than a complete list, but it gives a flavour of the common themes:

Il (Anglo-Saxon)
Furz-pig (England)
Vuzpeg (England)
Grainneog (Ireland)
Crainneag (Scotland)
Draenog (Wales)
Iddy-oddies (UK)
Urchin (UK)
Pindsvin (Denmark)
Hérrison (France)
Igel (Germany)
Egel (Holland)
Riccio (Italy)
Piggsvin (Norway)
Ouriço (Portugal)
Erizo (Spain)
Igelkott (Sweden)
Iriq (Albania)
Jež (Croatia)
Jezek (Czech
    Republic)
Siil (Estonia)
Siili (Finland)

Sündiszn̄ó
    (Hungary)
Jeż (Poland)
Arici (Romania)
Yozh (Russia)
Yizhak (Ukraine)
Kirpi (Turkey)
Ci wei (China)
Harinezumi (Japan
    – one online
    dictionary also
    had hejjihoggu)
Landak (Indonesia)
Qunfud (Arabic)
Hotchi-pig (Gypsy)
SeI (Hindi – also
    aik parkar ka
    jangli chuha,
    which apparently
    means 'spiky
    kind of mouse')
Kalunguyeye/
    Nungunungu
    (Swahili)

Whatever they are called, they are frequently labelled as fleabags. That is another on the list of regular questions – why have hedgehogs got so many fleas? And then there is also the accusation that the hedgehog has infested a dog.

But hedgehog fleas are more sensible than people give them credit for, being very particular. They are species-specific. *Archaeopsylla erinacei*, as its name suggests, is a hedgehog flea. It has evolved to survive in an extraordinary environment. Imagine life on the back of a rabbit, for example. The dense fur requires a special set of skills to navigate. Consider the back of a hedgehog, how sparse and alien that would seem to a flea used to more claustrophobic surroundings. And likewise dogs and cats just fail to provide a suitable habitat for *Archaeopsylla erinacei*.

How many fleas? Well, no more than any other animal of comparable size – an average of around 100 fleas per hog. But I have come across many with none and there are hedgehog carers who have reported over 1,000 fleas on a poor individual.

So why are they considered fleabags? Well, I have talked with many people about this and have come up with four suggestions:

1. The most obvious hedgehogs are the ones out in the day and these are usually sickly. Sickly hedgehogs are less able to look after themselves and so are more likely to be infested with fleas.

2. The next most frequently observed hedgehogs are dead. If it is a recent casualty, the stranded fleas will be seeking a new host and will spring towards any warm-blooded passer-by, however unsuitable the pelage.

3. Spines are sparser than the fur of a rabbit, therefore any beasties living on the skin will be more obvious.

4. The first reaction of most hedgehogs to an approach from a human is to bristle. The spines erect as a defence, and in so doing the dark and light bands move against each other, creating what hedgehog expert Nigel Reeve so eloquently described as 'an impression of a seething infestation'.

There are other misconceptions surrounding the flea, principally that they have a symbiotic relationship with hedgehogs – that is, the hedgehogs need them as much as they need the hedgehogs. The flourishing, and flealess, hedgehog population of New Zealand argues well against this idea.

Most of what I know about hedgehogs has, in some way, been filtered through to me from Dr Pat Morris. Now retired, though even busier than before, Pat has written more about hedgehogs than anyone else in the world. *The New Hedgehog Book* – an updated version of his original – is a brilliant introduction to the hedgehog basics and there has hardly been a work published on hedgehogs that does not draw heavily on his groundbreaking publications. It's easy not to be scrupulous in acknowledging sources, so I thought I'd do it upfront.

So there you have it, all the basic facts about hedgehogs. What's the rest of this book about, you may quite reasonably ask. Well, one part of it is to do with *Hemiechinus hughi*, a species I first read about fifteen years ago – though it took until now for the penny to drop that this hedgehog might possibly be called, as in fact it is, Hugh's hedgehog. Sometimes I really do wonder how I have managed to get as far as I have if I fail to spot the bleeding obvious.

And so from hedgehog facts to hedgehog love – because from here on in the book is about my, and many other people's, love affair with this remarkable animal. It is rare that an affair, begun as a teenager, lasts a lifetime, but I have been very lucky. Love affairs do not spring out of nowhere, there has to be a seduction, and my experience was no different.

CHAPTER
TWO

*What
Do
Hedgehogs
Do?*

Love did not blossom immediately. I suppose in the beginning we had more of a friendship and a working relationship. But I want to jump forward to the juicy bits.

The change came as I trudged the night fantastic through the Devon countryside on my first radio-tracking study. Perhaps it was the long period of isolation. Perhaps it was the chance to get to know hedgehogs individually. Whatever the reason, I ended up on my hands and knees, nose to nose with my new love. I like to think that my time with hedgehogs has brought me down to earth. Nocturnal adventures in hedgerows and ditches, searching for, to begin with, my subjects and later my friends, have left me damp, muddy and happy (most of the time).

Previous work had required me to rely on luck to find my hedgehogs, but this time they were all tagged and I was meeting each of them three or four times a night, getting to appreciate their very individual characters. Now, that might strike you as odd. I appreciate that some animals just don't do 'character' very much. After you have seen one bank vole, field vole, field mouse or harvest mouse, you have pretty much seen them all. I have met quite a few of these rodents in my time, usually rather indignant ones in live traps, but all the same, even on close inspection and, when I had been out on my own too long with too little sleep, after the odd conversation, really, there's very little sign of depth of character.

But if you do get the chance, you will find, as I have done, that there is more to a hedgehog than a snuffling bundle of spines. After all, you cannot deny that dogs and cats have individual characters, so why should it be hard to imagine the same for hedgehogs?

A big part of the problem, I believe, is point of view. It is easy to get nose to nose with dogs, but nose to nose with a hedgehog takes a little more trouble. Still, when you take that trouble you find something extraordinary.

The delight is that very swiftly differences in hedgehog character emerge. Some are bold; others are shy. Some are friendly; others are quite grumpy. Some will swiftly learn you are no threat and just run; others will always retreat into a ball. Some friendly hedgehogs have bad nights – there is no guarantee. In fact, one of the complications of hedgehog research is the difficulty in reaching broad generalizations about the beast.

Nevertheless, that is what I was trying to do, back in 1993, having been recruited to a damp and muddy caravan listing slightly at the top of a Devon field by hedgehog guru Pat Morris. This was the concluding chapter of a long piece of research he had been running, considering the slightly awkward question of whether there was any point in people looking after hedgehogs.

The question is awkward because there are a

lot of people who obviously get a great deal of pleasure from looking after sick and injured hogs, restoring them to health and then releasing the renovated bundles back into the wild. But until Pat started his work, no one had looked at how well the refurbished hogs survived.

Pat had already shown that adult hedgehogs, nursed back to health, cope very well when returned to the wild, though one of his hogs was unfortunately run over right by the sign leading into the Essex town of Dedham. We were looking at the most vulnerable group, juveniles, and in particular the autumn orphans, those young hedgehogs taken into care in their droves when they are found wandering forlornly in the run-up to hibernation.

Hedgehogs, four or five per litter, are usually born in June and early July, after a four-and-a-half-week gestation, but there can be second, or late, litters, resulting in young emerging much further into the year.

These late arrivals have a very poor chance of survival as they simply do not have enough time to put on the necessary weight to live through hibernation. They will often be seen out during the day as they try to cram in extra time to feed. If they look drunk, then they have the onset of hypothermia and are going to die unless looked after. Most of these hedgehogs are not really orphans, as hedgehog parenting is a pretty limited affair – the father has no part to play in their upbringing and after six weeks the mother gives them the heave-ho – but it is a useful shorthand for the youngsters that are in such a parlous state.

If hedgehogs enter hibernation weighing less than about 450 grams, they will die. The main problem they face is a lack of brown fat. There are two sorts of fat being laid down by hedgehogs as they prepare to hibernate. White fat is the basic day-to-day fat that keeps the animal alive, ticking over the metabolism at a remarkably low level: heartbeats down to five per minute and periods without drawing breath of up to nearly an hour. The physiology of the hibernating hedgehog is fascinating. The blood changes, the nervous system changes, the hormonal system changes. In fact, it can be hard to tell whether a hedgehog is hibernating or dead just by looking at it. If you find a hedgehog in the winter it is best to simply re-cover it with vegetation, but should you need to know whether it is alive, then stroke the spines. There ought to be a bristling response. Unfortunately, too many disturbances will prematurely use up the other sort of fat, brown fat. This is the starter motor and its absence will leave the hedgehog torpid until death.

Hedgehogs do not need to hibernate. It is just a survival strategy, so if there is no reason to – that is, if there is plenty of food available – they will stay wide awake. On the North Island of New Zealand, for example, hedgehogs rarely hibernate, or do so only briefly. And when hibernating, it is not a constant state of torpor. They might get up and have a wander, especially when the winters are mild.

Talking to wildlife carers and hedgehog rescuers around the UK, there is near unanimity in the observations of a distinct change in hedgehog behaviour: hedgehogs are spending less time in hibernation, if they are hibernating at all. Carers are being brought active hogs all winter long; one even had a baby brought in in January. That is not to say that hedgehogs have stopped hibernating – you still need to check any winter bonfires for sleeping hogs before ignition – just that phenology, the study of nature's rhythms, can indicate changes in the environment, perhaps before we even feel them. Is the world warming up? We may not notice a subtle shift of a fraction of a degree, but hedgehogs might.

The strategy of hibernation is employed not because hedgehogs themselves cannot survive the weather, but because their invertebrate food vanishes out of reach. This is also true of other species of hedgehog living in very different environments. For example, African desert hedgehogs' main threat to survival is not the cold, but the heat. And the reaction is not hibern[winter]ation, but aestiv[summer]ation.

To find out how well these rescued orphans survive, my job was to spend a couple of months following twelve that had spent the winter – proving hedgehogs do not need to hibernate – feasting at the RSPCA wildlife hospital at West Hatch in Somerset. Some of them were really rather rotund by the time I arrived.

Rescued orphans are very naive. They have no opportunity to learn the ropes of hedgehog life under the watchful eye of a mother. Would they be able to rely on instinct when confronted with their new home? Would they be able to find food, build nests and interact with other hedgehogs in a normal hedgehoggy way?

All the animals to be released had been found

the previous autumn – juveniles too small to survive hibernation. Nigel – yes, I named all twelve – had been wandering around in daytime in late September, weighing less than 100 grams, near a nest damaged by a mower. He would certainly have died if he had not been taken into care. Some of the others had had an even worse start. Hettie had been found in October with one of those wretched plastic rings used for holding cans in four-packs stuck round her middle. As she had grown, it had cut into her flesh and the wound had become infested with maggots. It is such a simple thing to cut up those bits of plastic before putting them into the bin – and it can save lives of so many animals, not just hedgehogs.

Each of my twelve, and I very quickly became proprietorial, had a small radio transmitter attached to a patch of clipped spines on their back. The transmitter included a luminous tag, which glowed green and was invaluable in helping to find the hedgehogs – though it was potentially alarming for the uninitiated to see little green lights travelling through gardens and fields.

We released the animals in two batches. The first was simply let go. The second was provided with food and bedding and kept in pre-release cages for five days. The cages were then opened, but food and bedding were placed in them for another five days, giving the hedgehogs somewhere to retreat if they failed to acclimatize in the wild. We already know that some species, such as dormice, need to be treated like this and if we found hedgehogs benefited, then we could pass the experience on to the thousands of hedgehog rescuers around the country. Our results showed that there was little difference in how hedgehogs fared in the two groups. This is encouraging, as most people just release hedgehogs into the wild following time in care.

Nigel and Hettie were both released in the second batch. Hettie had a more subdued, though no less endearing character. She would remain quite relaxed when picked up for her nightly weighing session – a brief indignity involving the animal being placed in a converted pillowcase hooked beneath a spring balance. Keeping a record of the weight was an essential part of the study, because we needed to know if the newly released hedgehogs were eating properly (if they weren't, they would lose weight very rapidly). This would not only indicate their wellbeing, but also give us an idea if the hedgehogs were coping with the new environment.

Given the naivety of these animals, I was worried that the seven months of cosseting they had received might have affected their ability to cope with life in the wild. And if the answer to my study was that they really were unable to reintegrate into hedgehog society after such intensive care, this would question whether there was any point to it in the first place.

If only the caravan had been a little warmer. But at least the Calor gas stove helped melt the ice on the windows as I cooked yet another pan of brown rice and vegetables for my dinner.

While on the subject of eating, I met David Bellamy and, as one does, got around to talking about hedgehogs and he revealed something that might shock his once loyal audience. Professor Bellamy is a self-confessed hedgehog eater.

Actually, eating hedgehogs is not such a problem. His was roadkill cooked with a stuffing of wild herbs. And even though I have not eaten meat for over twenty years, I can see the logic of not allowing good protein to go to waste. Perhaps one day . . . Maybe it would mark a true coming together of the hedgehog and me?

It is one of the most repeated stories that surround hedgehogs – 'The Gypsies eat them, don't they?' The story goes that you wrap the hedgehog in clay and then cook it in an oven, or perhaps in a fire. When the meat is done you just crack open the newly fired pot and the spines magically come away from the flesh. But is this really true?

I have read that this method of cooking, unless done in a very large fire, will result in a soggy mess. One school of thought is that it's best to chop the hedgehog up to use in a recipe, as Arthur Boyt described in the *Guardian* in 2006:

Hedgehog spaghetti carbonara
(serves four)

500g spaghetti, 30ml olive oil, 250g lean hedgehog,
1 medium onion (chopped), 125ml water, 60ml
dry white wine, 4 eggs, 60ml double cream, 100g
grated Parmesan cheese

- chop hedgehog into small chunks

- beat eggs and cream together in a bowl, and add half the Parmesan cheese

- put pasta in boiling water

- put onions and hedgehog chunks in pan
with olive oil on medium heat until onions are
almost clear

- add wine and reduce heat

- drain pasta when cooked, and combine it
with egg, cream and cheese mix

- add meat, onions and wine without draining
fat and mix thoroughly

- garnish with remaining Parmesan

- serve immediately

Arthur specializes in cooking up roadkill. In fact, it sounds like
he will eat pretty much anything he finds (the Labrador had no
collar – and tasted a bit like lamb). But not all hedgehog eaters
are clearing up after the murderous rampage of the motorcar. I
came across a debate on a website dedicated to hunting wildlife
where one contributor talked of meeting travellers who had
bred a strain of terrier specifically for catching hedgehogs. He
described the hedgehog meal he was given as 'a bit greasy but
OK white meat a bit like young rabbit, but I reckon you'd
need one per person . . .'

I got an email from Alan Birks describing his post-war experience
with hedgehogs while on holiday as a child in Rhyl when he made
friends with a Gypsy boy who invited him back for supper:

They asked me if I had ever tasted hedgehog and then began to prepare it. I do not know how they killed it but they had a brick oven in the garden and they covered the hedgehog in clay and put it in the oven. Some time later they cracked open the clay and all the spines remained attached to the clay. I was unsure but I tasted it and it tasted like watery chicken.

Evidence of hedgehog eating goes way back. In 1699 Jezreel Jones published 'An Account of the Moorish Way of Dressing Their Meat' in the learned journal *Philosophical Transactions*:

The Hedgehog is a Princely Dish amongst them, and before they kill him, rub his Back against the Ground, by holding its Feet betwixt two, as Men do a Saw that saws Stones, till it has done squeaking; then they cut its Throat, and with a Knife cut off all its Spines and singe it. They take out its Guts, stuff the Body with some Rice, sweet Herbs, Garavancas, Spice, and Onions; they put some Butter and Garavancas into the Water they stew it in, and let it stew in a little Pot, close stopped, till it is enough, and it proves an excellent Dish.

Earlier still, according to experimental archaeologist Jacqui Wood, hedgehogs would have formed a part of prehistoric diet. She told me:

Clay baking is the most effective way of cooking hedgehogs or small birds, as you do not have to bother with the spines or the feathers. When baked they come away from the flesh beautifully. The only experiments I have done with hedgehogs are with fresh roadkill, so I know it does work and they do taste like pork, hence the hog in the name.

Back to Nigel, Hettie and the rest of the team. To get to know them I had to adopt their lifestyle, up to a point – I might be fond of them, but I was not up for sharing their dinner. For two months I would poke my nose out into the world as the sun fell, curling up to sleep when it rose.

And the more time I spent with the hedgehogs, the more it became clear that their allotted identification numbers, which were in fact the frequencies of the radio transmitters attached to their backs, were too formal. So to the pressing matter of naming hedgehogs.

After the first few days, when it became clear that number 288 liked to disappear at great speed, Nigel was named after a not so proficient racing driver. He would cause me confusion by making it from one end of a field to the other before me. I would see a green glow, get excited at an easy catch (sometimes it took ages to track down a hedgehog) and then find it was Nigel, again.

He was a very useful hedgehog. Not only was he busy, he was also very accepting of my presence and began to allow me into his world. One night I followed him out on a hunting expedition. Down the quiet lane he jogged – I was required to walk at a reasonable pace to keep up. Every now and then he swooped on an unsuspecting morsel, usually so fast that I could not see what he was eating. Eventually I got a glimpse – small slugs. I am often tackled on the subject of slugs: people will tell me that they have hedgehogs in their garden, but there are also still slugs.

Well, there is a thing about slugs – not all of them are bad. We are well aware of the chaos that evil slugs can wreak in a bed of carefully nurtured seedlings, but we are less aware of the wonderful things that other slugs, the detritivores, get up to. You may have heard tell of the wonders performed by dung beetles – and the idea that if it were not for them Africa would be knee deep in Elephant poo. Well, some slugs do similar, if less dramatic, work around the garden, aiding the decomposition of leaf litter. So before you set about the complete eradication of slugs, consider the consequences, and also consider that you will be removing lots of hedgehog food as well.

Many of the slugs that the likes of Nigel are gobbling will be small, but the slugs we are likely to see around the garden are the great big slime monsters. I have a habit of walking around barefoot when the weather is nice and there is little as unpleasant as treading on a slug – the slime is persistent (one piece of advice I heard was to try shaving it off).

Back to Nigel: he found a black slug that was rather larger than any I had seen him tackle so far. Scrabbling at it, he rolled it back and forth across the tarmac and then he ate it. After he moved off, I examined the ground and found

it was covered with slug slime. It looked like he had been deliberately removing the unpleasant mucilage to make the slug more palatable. I have seen blackbirds do something similar, wiping a slug on the pavement.

I suspect the tactic didn't work, because his next point of call was a dandelion leaf, which he avidly 'mouthed' before spitting it out. Nigel then started smacking his lips and contorting himself in his efforts to spread a froth of saliva on to his spines – a wonderful display of self-anointing.

Such an unusual noise was coming from Nigel that I pulled my recording equipment out and stuck my microphone close to him – you shouldn't leave home without one, as you never know when it might be needed. His response was to puff himself up and snort. Though this aggressive display did have the desired effect of making the microphone retreat, it also provided some wonderful noises for the tape.

While self-anointing is usually associated with particularly strong flavours, there is no specific chemical that sets it off. It has been prompted by distilled water. I have seen it when people wearing perfume, or who have washed their hands in scented soap, have handled hedgehogs, but the most frequently quoted stimulus is an old leather shoe.

Why? No one knows for sure. Each idea seems plausible up to a point – but then fails. Perhaps it is an attempt to rid themselves of fleas, yet flea-free hedgehogs do it. Or to coat the spines with a toxin, to make the hedgehog more repellent to potential predators, but it can be caused by the most innocuous of substances. Perhaps it is a device for disseminating scent more effectively. This, so far, seems the best theory and other mammals are known to have scent carried in saliva. The surface area afforded by the spines would give a great platform from which evaporation could occur.

So Nigel was hunting – he was eating – and this was great news. The first thing to show a problem in a released hedgehog will be a failure to eat, at which point they will start to lose weight. That is why checking the hedgehogs' weight each night was so important, even if getting tipped into a modified pillow-case and dangled beneath a spring balance was not particularly elegant.

The other key piece of data I was collecting was the location of the day nest. This served two purposes: it gave me a better idea of where to start looking as the next  night began and also revealed how well the animals were coping in their new environment. Not as simple as weight loss, but if a hedgehog either used one nest all the time or kept making a new one every morning, well, this would be abnormal behaviour, suggesting that something was wrong, perhaps that the time in captivity had affected their ability to nest properly.

Some nests I have seen are as intricate as a bird's. Hogs make two sorts of nest: the day-to-day day nest and the more substantial hibernaculum. The day nest can be pretty flimsy, depending on the weather. I have found healthy hedgehogs covered in little more than a scattering of leaves. Others have made quite a serious effort, pulling vast amounts of vegetation with their mouths into a thicket of brambles. The combing effect of a rotating hedgehog should not be underestimated.

The hibernaculum, on the other hand, is a far more substantial construction, 50 centimetres in diameter, with walls of leaves up to 10 centimetres thick. Pat Morris found that good nests can be fantastically well insulated, keeping the internal temperature between 1 and 5 degrees centigrade while the outside temperature fluctuates between −8 and +10. Avoiding frostbite is an obvious need, but it is equally important that brief rises in temperature do not arouse the hedgehog prematurely.

Similar qualities of insulation would have been appreciated in my caravan. At least it kept the rain out – it seemed to rain on every single day of the first month of the project and the radio-tracking receiver had a warning on it in bold letters: DO NOT EXPOSE TO MOISTURE. When it got wet, it stopped working.

But there were nights when everything worked wonderfully. Or at least the kit did. The hedgehogs were, as it soon became apparent, a law unto themselves.

Hedgehog number 298 had vanished. It was only her second night out and she was nowhere to be seen or heard. The radio receiver I was carrying picked up nothing but static, with the occasional, tantalizing respite hinting that there might be a firmer signal if I just went a bit closer to where I did not want to go.

The farm I was based on was set on the side of a luxuriant valley. When I first arrived, I decided to 'beat the bounds' and went walking around the perimeter. Up the steep hill south of the farm, I found a badger latrine and, just like in the field guides, there was a snag of badger hair caught on a nearby piece of barbed wire. Minutes later I disturbed a hare and then a buzzard appeared overhead. At first I thought it must be a seagull – the noise felt out of place in the rolling valleys.

Arcadia ... almost. This otherwise idyllic landscape had a rather substantial blot: enormous 400-kilovolt-carrying pylons striding through the valley like the frozen skeletons of giant robots. And there was a son et lumière in full swing as I reluctantly plodded on towards 298 in the dark, damp night.

The air buzzed and crackled with electricity. This was the closest I had ever been to such pylons and I was totally unprepared for the way they acted when the air was wet. Starting with an electrical hum, the cables rapidly moved on to a cacophony of crackling as the air got wetter, until they eventually began to glow. As they did now.

All this might have been OK if the pylons carrying the cables had not slouched in their duty and held them more loftily. But the steep valley forced the crackling, glowing cables and the hedgehog tracker rather closer together than at least one party cared for.

So early in the project and I was already talking to myself: muttering abuse at the absconding hedgehog, thinking of a name that was even remotely polite for her and trying to calm myself. The noise and proximity of the cables were bad enough, but what really set me gibbering was the aerial I was carrying. I must have slept through the lesson in physics where they explained the dos and don'ts of high-voltage electricity play. It seemed logical that any self-respecting chunk of electricity would home in on the attractive metal rod I held above my head and fry me.

By the time I found 298, I had calmed down enough to think of something suitable to mark her exploratory prowess. Dame Freya Stark, the 'passionate nomad', seemed like the sort of person to associate with this determinedly mobile hog.

I did what I needed to, separating the great lady from her worm, weighed her, double-checked that 298 really was a female, then let her return to the business of tormenting me. True to form, two nights later she went missing again, in the opposite direction.

Males are supposed to travel further and faster than females, but as with all things hedgehog, it can be hard to generalize, and, by the end of this project, it was the females who had undertaken the longest journeys. Researchers have shown that, on average, male hedgehogs will travel 2–3 kilometres a night. Some will travel only a few hundred metres and may stay within that range for their entire lives; others have been recorded to move up to 4 kilometres in a single night. Females, just not my females, have been reported to average slightly over half this distance.

It all depends on when you do the study, though. In the spring, male hedgehogs are up and out, looking for a mate, and travel widely. In the autumn, it is the females who tend to be the most active, as they make up for the time lost rearing young, feeding and fattening for hibernation.

I eventually tracked Freya to the far end of the valley, over a kilometre from where she was released and two from where she was torturing me with pylon anxiety. These are

just the distances on the map and mean nothing to a hedgehog, which is rarely able to walk anywhere in a straight line; there are always distractions for a busy nose.

This time she had ended up in the barn of a farm and I was given my first opportunity to have the 'Excuse me, but one of my hedgehogs is missing . . .' conversation. The farmer was genuinely interested, which was just as well, because Freya hung around for a week before returning closer to the release site.

Fortunately not all the hedgehogs behaved like this. Hettie remained near the farm where she was released, at least early on, frequently foraging in the garden. Nigel exhibited very different habits. He travelled much further than any of the other animals, but regularly returned to the same day nest, spending only the odd 'night' at different sites. Hettie, by comparison, spent no more than five at each nest she had built. How much this represents a difference between sexes or just between individuals is hard to tell.

Over the weeks, they all became far more relaxed about being handled. This gave me wonderful opportunities to look at them closely. But with their new-found confidence, they no longer curled into compliant balls of spines when I needed to pick them up for weighing. Instead, they would run away whenever they got the chance.

When a hedgehog decides to run it undergoes a transformation almost as fundamental as the ball-rolling escape. The loose 'skirt' is hitched up, like a car altering its suspension; the body is lifted off the ground and away it goes. Top speed has been reported as 9 km/h, but, as with the cheetah, these extraordinary bursts are only maintained for a short while. Then the skirt lowers and they return to the clockwork gait (the hedgehog, not the cheetah. I met a couple of tame cheetahs in Namibia. The youngster was rather haughty and the adult a bit of a lapdog. Neither of them was as fascinating as the wonderful hedgehog.)

So did they run from me because they recognized my smell? Had my repeatedly benign interventions in their lives made them less fearful of humans? Perhaps I was beginning to smell like one of them? Certainly my wax coat must have had a pretty hoggy aroma.

With them beetling off at top speed in the dark, it was a good job I had the additional assistance of the luminous tags. Radio-tracking is good at getting you to the area the hedgehog is in, but the fine-tuning is not perfect and the last few metres can be tortuous. You can't buy the tags any more. Something about them being radioactive – well, I didn't know that then. Perhaps too many hedgehogs in one place would create a critical mass? Or maybe terrorists would round them up to create a dirty bomb with biological shrapnel?

The tags were clearly visible, when the nights were very dark, from more than 50 metres. But there were hazards too. When the moon was bright, moondrops, glistening on dew-laden grass or reflected in puddles, became dead ringers for hedgehogs and sent me chasing spectres.

The moon was a great companion. Not a friend you could rely on, but one who was a great comfort when she arrived.

And there was little to compare with the delight of walking the fields trailing a moon shadow.

At the end of the project, Jean, who lived in the farmhouse, asked if I could leave the luminous tags on the hedgehogs because she was often kept awake at night by her knees. 'So I just take myself down to the kitchen, make a cup of tea and read,' she explained. 'Only now I am not even bothering to switch the light on – I just watch the show as the little green lights busy themselves around the garden.'

I would have loved to agree to her request, but at over £100 per transmitter, that was rather a lot to ask for.

Lights darting into the undergrowth were fun, but there was better on the way. On the lawn, where the grass was short enough for me to see from a distance, I sometimes observed an amazing dance of two sprites, one circling the other, with periodic leaps and sneezes like waltzing glow-worms with hay fever. This meant I was going to find two hedgehogs at once. I did feel a bit of a killjoy, though, as it seemed being dunked into the pillowcase did rather affect the ardour of these courting hedgehogs.

But the passion was not dampened too much, thank goodness, and my friends seemed quite able to recommence an active life later in the evening. On one night, I found Nigel with three different females in the space of four hours, and the following night, Hettie was found with two different males within an hour. All this promiscuity reassured me that my charges were becoming integrated into wild hedgehog society, as frequently the interactions included a wild hedgehog – one that was already resident on the farm.

Early on I met some of the other residents. But this time not hedgehogs. One particularly cold, clear and beautiful night, before I was able to find some non-leaking wellies and was resorting to shopping bags as a third pair of socks, I froze at what seemed, on this particularly silent night, like a ferocious commotion in the nearby hedge.

Before I could plan my retreat from whatever monsters were at work, out popped a black and russet badger (the soil gives everything in the area, including most of the content of my caravan, a ruddle tinge). After snorting back and forth a few metres from me, it disappeared, only to reappear moments later, tumbling down the slope, rolling, grunting and snarling with another. The two fought in and out of the hedge, up and down the slope, for ten minutes before charging off up the hill. They had been so set on their game that they failed to notice the audience. Or perhaps the audience was beginning to smell so game that he blended into the landscape.

It was magical and only when I tried to move again did I realize how effective mind over matter can be. My feet had become so fed up with conditions that they had shut off communication with the rest of my body and gone on strike. By the time I made it back up the other side of the valley I was shivering uncontrollably and went to sleep still in my thermal underwear, in two sleeping bags and wearing a woolly hat.

Normally it rained.

Sometimes it was little more than heavy fog, droplets of water only just heavy enough to fall, and so small they penetrated every possible corner. My beard was a sponge, needing to be wrung. Other times it was real rain, descending torrents like the powerful chords in the finale of Bruckner's Fourth Symphony.

Dragging myself back out to work after a cup of tea was hard enough given the wet, but there was something deeply counterintuitive about getting active as 'Sailing By' drifts from the radio. However, it almost always seemed worthwhile, a bit like jumping into a river; you might hang around on the edge for ages, but you don't regret jumping.

Jumping into a sensual feast. After the cold, damp and dark, skies and spirits begin to lighten. There was a sense of spring loitering. Blossom and new leaves, brave bumblebees and the conversations of birds getting louder and more confident.

During the day, the hedge banks were lit with dog violets, early purple orchids, garlic mustard, stitchwort and dandelions. By night, the moon reflected from these plants, highlighting the track. And as the weeks passed, the pastel shades of primroses gave way to the egg-yolk yellow of dandelions. The scent of spring; now that would be worth bottling.

Out at night I would move through a wash of wild garlic down the lane, up into the wood where a wall of bluebells waited, out of the woods on to the drier slopes to be greeted with waves of coconut from the thickets of gorse. Might leave the dog fox out of the bottle though.

Every hour or so I was reminded that I was in the present day by the noise of a car travelling along the small lane that ran by the farm. Searchlights would scour the bottoms of clouds as the cars pulled up a steep hill. However, even these occasional and slow-moving cars proved their might in the face of the most dogged hedgehog defence.

Cars killed two of my hogs. Jimmy was the first and then Billy. Billy was great; he seemed to really relish being handled, while still acting like a normal hedgehog out in the field. He would snuffle around my already filthy clothing, trying to get up sleeves and into pockets. I should have thanked him for that; I am sure this coating of *eau d'hérrison* aided my acceptance by his compatriots.

There is no teaching some of them, though, and it was not long after the death of Billy that I had one of a series of moments of high anxiety. The disadvantages of becoming too fond of your study animal dawned on me.

Hettie vanished. I had caught up with her earlier in the evening over the hill to the north of the farm. This was unusual territory for her; she had been consistently around the central area for the past six weeks. When I went back to get a final fix on her, there was not a dicky bird, just the white noise of static from the radio receiver.

If she had continued in a straight line from where I last saw her, the destination was depressingly clear. From the crest of the hill you looked down on the nearest busy road. Still no signal as I approached the road – a good sign, as the transmitter at least should survive a squashing. Up to the crest of the hill to the east and again, nothing. That was an early lesson in the art of radio-tracking: elevation, elevation, elevation. Getting the aerial a little higher could make all the difference to the beeps on my machine.

So I headed west, deeply concerned that at any moment I was going to come across the flattened corpse of the sweet-natured hedgehog.

Traffic was beginning to increase heading east to Taunton and beyond. Though I noticed the cars were behaving oddly. As they got closer to me they slowed, then pulled out into the middle of the road, accelerating away. What was it about me that was causing the consternation? The head torch on the woolly hat that failed to control the unruly hair? The mud-covered boots, trousers and coat? The bag full of paints, notebooks and scales? The box of electronics? The large TV aerial? Or was it the look of a man deeply tormented by the realization that at any moment he was going to find a flattened friend?

 Then the faintest signal, a lone beep. I walked faster and the beeps became clearer and louder, though still from the road. As I reached a small farmhouse, right on the road, the signal was so strong that I knew she was around there somewhere. And not on the road. A great feeling of relief rushed over me, but I had to stop. I really did not want to go poking around a stranger's farm while everyone was still asleep. Too many close encounters with territorial dogs have taught me well.

So, sure she was OK, I headed home for a nap. I was off familiar ground and decided to risk a short cut. The sun was teasing the few clouds and I was enjoying just being outside, so it was a shame to waste this walk on tarmac.

I startled a small herd of red deer on the far side of a field, then, to my astonishment, they vanished. Was I that tired? I kept on towards where they had been. The hedge looked solid, but as I got closer I found the deer's gap. I pushed through the small breach and entered another world.

There were two lines of trees that had grown over, creating a verdant tunnel. The passage between them was sunken. I had entered a 'green lane'. Green lanes are relics of our transport history – they are the old, often redundant routes that have somehow managed to evade the depredations of modern life. This short green tunnel was once part of the main track over the hill. The sunken nature paid tribute to the thousands of feet that had passed that way.

Most green lanes have been destroyed, either through development or neglect. This one was safe, even if only a segment remains. People rarely passed this way – not just from the absence of footprints, but also from the absence of rubbish.

Try a short cut, walk, slowly, off the beaten track and allow yourself to get a little bit lost. I like that feeling, not knowing where I am but pretty sure of where I am going. It allows you a chance to get much closer to nature. So go poke your nose behind hedges; you never know what you might find.

I could have wallowed in the beauty of it all for hours, but it was a long time since I was last asleep – and unless I was going to curl up against the ancient hedge bank, I had to keep moving. I wonder what dreams might have percolated through the soil?

Returning to the farm at 10 a.m. after a couple of hours' sleep, I introduced myself at the house and acquired the eager assistance of two young helpers, Denise and Kevin. We all searched among the remnants of old cars and farm machinery. Finally, after scrabbling through some undergrowth, the nest was found in the middle of a hedge. As I emerged, looking like I had been dragged through a hedge backwards (which was almost true), Denise passed judgement: 'We don't get many people like you down here.'

Hettie required me to change my routine, as I now had to make sure I got to her while Denise and Kevin were still up. They were furious if I ever failed to get them out on the hunt.

Soon after Hettie disappeared over the horizon, Hannah also did a 'runner', turning up at a farm about a kilometre north of the release farm. Again, the owners were very accommodating, if slightly bemused, as I wandered around their immaculate garden searching for clear bleeps. Sure enough, Hannah had made herself quite at home in a barn. What was going on? The males, not the females, were supposed to be the wanderers, searching far afield for female conquests.

A possible answer was revealed when the vet came to do an interim health check on the hedgehogs. Hettie and Hannah were pregnant. Perhaps they had left 'home' in an attempt to escape the relative overcrowding of the study site, before giving birth to their babies – the best present any rehabilitation study could hope for.

As the project began to draw to a close in mid-May, I took a detour from my regular work. I had been asked to appear on live TV, radio-tracking hedgehogs around a golf course in Nottingham for a show called *Nightshift*. I was so excited, but what a rude introduction to the reality of this sort of reality television.

For my first bit to camera I had to stand with the radio-tracking gear, holding my stunt hedgehog. After a brief interview I put the hedgehog on the ground and off we went. As soon as the cameras stopped, I had to pick up the hedgehog and pop it back in its box. Then, three hours later, I was back out with my beast, in exactly the same place, only this time with the cameras and lights facing in the opposite direction. I put the hedgehog down again and made up a story of the foraging it had been doing in the intervening period. Now, I am sure that this was a one-off and that the BBC would never stoop so low again.

And I never got to apologize to the staff at the five-star hotel I was put up in – it was probably the first time they had ever had a hedgehog spend a couple of nights. He was in a box in the bathroom and helped remind me why the European hedgehog is such an unsuitable pet – they stink.

On my return to Devon, Peter, the farmer, was obviously quite agitated about something. Pat Morris had come to check up on how things were going, so we were led into the hayfield wondering what on earth had got into the previously calm farmer. As we got into the field he told us that he had found the remains of a hedgehog.

It was not difficult to find. There was a large area of flattened hay with plenty of congealed blood – and in the midst of the gore, the skin and spines of the hedgehog. It had been emptied out.

Pat and I bent down to investigate. Well, the good news was that it was not one of 'ours'. It was a wild hedgehog – a resident of the area that I had marked with paint on its spines earlier in the project. But the bad news was that this looked like the work of a badger.

Now, we knew that there were badgers in the area – in fact, it is pretty much impossible to find anywhere in the West Country without badgers. And while badgers are known predators of hedgehogs, they are also competitors – meaning that this site was at least going to provide plenty of food for our charges.

This is a great bit of ecology, called intra-guild predation. It's not often that you get to equate the hedgehog with the hyena, but I'll give it a go. Hedgehogs and badgers are of the same 'guild'; they eat the same sorts of thing. They are competitors for worms and other invertebrate prey. Hyenas and lions are of the same 'guild'; they eat the same sorts of thing. They are competitors for ungulates and other vertebrate prey. And here is the link: lions also eat hyenas and badgers eat hedgehogs, but not all the time. By eating hedgehogs, badgers are also removing competitors for the limited supply of worms.

We had taken the chance to use this farm simply because it had been used by the RSPCA for a number of years as a release point for hedgehogs. And while there had been no formal follow-up, there was clearly a healthy resident population now

– and as we had just discovered, when a badger tucks into a hedgehog, it is fairly clear to see.

So it was with a degree of trepidation that Pat and I set out that night. We had tracked down all but two – Freya and Nigel. Both being fairly active, this was not unexpected. As I had been away for a few days, I was worried that they might have disappeared from the range of the receiver.

Eventually I got a signal from Freya – and it was coming from a part of the farm that she had rarely frequented. It was a muddled series of beeps. Something felt not quite right, but I was not prepared for the shock of what confronted me tucked in among the exposed roots of an unkempt hedge. There she was, just her spines, with the transmitter still attached, merrily beeping away.

A few weeks later, after I returned to civilization, I was to get an even greater shock. I read an obituary for Dame Freya Stark. My hedgehog's namesake had died on 9 May 1993 at the age of 100 – the very same day that I had found Freya eaten by a badger.

So to Nigel. There are good scientific reasons for not having favourites when attempting to conduct an experiment. And there are good practical reasons. I was a nervous wreck as we eventually caught a signal. Would my mate be in the same state as Freya?

The signal got clearer. At last we were on the right path and my spirits rose as it led us to an area he was obviously fond of. Getting closer, the volume of the beeping rose until it was distorting on the small speaker. I was on top of him and there he was. I saw the glow of the tag, crouched down to scoop him up, ready to hug the living daylights out of the poor beast, only to find that I had hold of the husk of my friend.

Retiring to the caravan, Pat and I sat in despondent silence as we nursed our tea. Though I have to say that while I mourned the passing of dear friends, I think Pat was mourning the loss of good data. After a while we began to try to work out what was happening. Why should there be no problem with badgers for six weeks and then, in just a few days, carnage had been let loose? We came up with a theory that still seems the most reasonable. The resident badger population did not seem to eat hedgehogs, so perhaps this was the work of a passing badger – one that was looking for a new territory. We reasoned it was quite possible that hedgehogs only become food to badgers once they have learned the bundle of prickles is worth dealing with – perhaps after coming upon a casualty on the roads.

Pat left me to complete the work and at around 2.45 a.m. I headed back into the night as he headed back to his warm bed and breakfast. My remaining hedgehogs were soon all accounted for, apart from Little Willy. He was one of the smallest hedgehogs, did not often stray and had earned his name from the detumescence of an injury to his more sensitive parts. Earlier in the night I had found him moving up towards the south border of the farm, so it seemed likely that he had simply plucked up the courage to take a grand detour from his otherwise relatively sedentary lifestyle.

As the signal got clearer, it seemed that he was still on the move – a very good thing, as I was fed up with losing hedgehogs. And then, as I caught sight of the luminous tag, I also heard him eating. Hedgehogs can be very noisy eaters. I pulled out my tape recorder and started to describe the evening's events and how I was glad to be able to track down this last hedgehog. But slowly it dawned on me that the noise was not Little Willy eating – but of Little Willy being eaten. I pushed through the brambles, startling the voracious badger and being confronted with the gruesome remnants of another hedgehog. His head was still largely intact, but other than that there were only spines and the transmitter. That made quite an interesting bit of radio.

The atmosphere changed for me. For the final ten days of work, every excursion into the night was filled with a sense of dread. Unwisely I had switched my affection to George. Standoffish to begin with, he had mellowed and was just a fine solid hog. Wandering around with my tape recorder running, I tried to capture the essence of a night's work, not realizing the drama I was about to capture. Everything had been going fine until it came to finding George. Conservative to a fault, he had a routine, and he had slipped out of it. The signal was mixed; perhaps he was close to a building. I couldn't help myself as the anxiety rose, my voice tightened and tears began to well up as I stumbled through gates and across fields. But then the elation at finding him in one piece was so heartfelt, all honestly caught on tape.

A few months later, after my rather embarrassing loss of control had been broadcast on the radio, I was introduced to a record producer at a party. He was, I was surprised to find, excited to meet me. He had heard the broadcast and was so taken by the expressions of love I had for George that he wanted to sample it for a dance track ... If he did, I have never heard it, and having recently listened to myself again, I kind of hope he didn't.

So what can we conclude about the work? It was quite easy to forget, among the drama, that this was a serious piece of scientific study. We were trying to find out whether young hedgehogs, having been kept in captivity all winter, could cope with life in the wild. These were animals that had no previous experience of life in the wild, so would they be able to fend for themselves? Would they be able to find food? Would they be able to create their own nests? Would they be able to find them again?

At first sight, the statistics are rather grim. By the end of the study we knew that only four out of the initial twelve were alive. This would suggest a disaster and that the premise of the wildlife rehabilitators, who have been releasing hedgehogs like this for decades, was mistaken. After all, if there is only going to be a 33 per cent survival, you have to seriously look at the benefits to be gained from all the work.

 But it was not quite as bad as it first seemed. We lost two transmitters, but these animals may well have survived and the fact that their corpses did not turn up, either as badger snack or roadkill, is encouraging. And of the remaining six, two were killed by cars and badgers killed three. Neither of these causes can be blamed on the rehabilitation the hedgehogs experienced with the RSPCA. We found wild hedgehogs in the area that had suffered just the same fates. That leaves only one who died when taken back into the care of the RSPCA very near the beginning of the experiment. He was a sickly animal and perhaps should not have been released in the first place.

We showed that rehabilitated hedgehogs behave in the same way as normal hedgehogs. They feed, sleep, fornicate and die just like a wild animal. So there is good news, and if hedgehogs are released in areas where there are no badgers, their chances of survival increase dramatically.

But it would be harder to control for cars. Now this piece of work made me think about hedgehogs and cars. Yes, they are seen dead on the roads more than any other animal. Though this is in part due to the fact that their spiny coat tends to remain visible for much longer than, say, a rabbit, which will be swiftly scavenged by crows and gulls, therefore giving the impression that the hedgehogs are much more frequently run over. But it was the density of traffic that really struck me. The two that were killed were squashed on roads where, at the time of their death, there was little more than one car every hour. So perhaps the absence of traffic gave the hedgehogs a false sense of security. Perhaps busier roads are just not attractive to a hungry hedgehog.

Whatever the answer, cars are still lethal contributors to our nation's ecology and I will keep to my bicycle as much as possible. And as for badgers? Well, there was a little part of me that gloated at the ludicrous badger cull being promoted by the UK government – that'll teach them to mess with my hedgehogs. But the reality is that hedgehogs and badgers have been playing out this scenario for many more years than we have been interfering.

I should point out that the naming of Nigel happened before I had ever heard of Nigel Reeve, which is a good job when you consider what happened to Freya Stark on the consumption of her namesake.

For me, there was no looking back. I had learned so much about the nature of hedgehogs, but had also been given a glimpse into the nature of being a hedgehog. Just before he died, I had my most memorable night out with Nigel. I had returned to my caravan, exhausted, at around 4 a.m. As I stepped out of the cold caravan into the relatively balmy night air to clean my teeth, there was Nigel, watching me.

He waited until I had finished before moving off towards the lane. I had a feeling that he wanted me to follow. So, with toothbrush in pocket, I set off after him.

It was a very special night. After three weeks of seemingly unending rain, it was mild and dry. But while there was no rain, the hedgehog's world must have been like a monsoon; the rich grass shed jewels of dew as he pushed through the undergrowth. Following a fearless Nigel forced me into this microcosm. Sheep-sized slugs and dew, like disco glitter balls, refracting moonbeams. But he had no eyes for this ephemeral brilliance. His world went in through his nose and that led him, snuffling, snorting and sniffing: hunting.

The noise of a hungry hedgehog is something to experience. No table manners are taught in the all too brief six-week induction to the world from mama. Nigel definitely chewed with his mouth wide open.

Risking life and limb, he chose to walk on the warm and dry tarmac, eschewing his natural habitat of cold, wet grass. I have short legs too and can appreciate this gamble. Maybe this is one of the reasons so many hedgehogs are killed on the road.

I have spent so long in the company of hedgehogs, but this hour with just the two of us, out at night together, caused a shift in my relationship with these animals. By now I was soaked and muddy, lying on the ground, observing the way he worked. He stopped, looked up at me and we both paused, nose to nose. We looked into each other's eyes and I swear there was a flicker of something.

And then he was off, and I was left feeling ever so slightly changed.

CHAPTER
THREE

*Hedgehogs
and
Birds*

Love affairs are rarely simple. And while I was happily falling for these unlikely sirens, there is a darker side to the story of our relationship with hedgehogs. In fact, my first 'professional' encounter with hedgehogs raised a disturbing question, one I had never previously considered: is it OK to like hedgehogs?

There is a divide, more profound, some might argue, than the schism between rugby league and rugby union or Catholics and Protestants. It is the split between those with a fulsome love of the natural world and bird fanatics.

Whether it is in Orkney, at the hands of gamekeepers, out on the Uists or down in New Zealand, the bird lovers have cast hedgehogs alongside such obvious rascals as cats and rats.

North Ronaldsay

While I might complain about the conflict, there is no denying that it is what got me started on the true path of hedgehog love. Though perhaps my thanks ought to go to a postman. He was only trying to find an environmentally friendly solution to the slugs in his greenhouse. He had no idea that the two hedgehogs he picked up in his aunt's garden in Inverness would have such an impact on his island.

The postman's delivery was in 1972. Thirteen years later the hedgehogs on North Ronaldsay were a menace. The national press reported that there were more than 100 hedgehogs for every person on the island – and there were only ninety people. The *Sunday Express* ran the headline 'A heaven for hedgehogs – island where two pets became 10,000'. The island of North Ronaldsay, the most northerly of the Orkneys, is just over 690 hectares, so that makes over fourteen hedgehogs per hectare. The best habitats on offer on the mainland can expect only one per hectare. So the islanders should have been tripping over these illegal immigrants.

The spiky interlopers were in the news because of their rapacious appetites: not only did they have an apparently rabbit-like ability to reproduce; they were accused of feasting on bird's eggs. North Ronaldsay is a birds' paradise, and if the hedgehogs were eating their eggs, then they had to go.

The local GP, Kevin Woodbridge, who was also the founder of the bird observatory, had been monitoring the breeding success of ground-nesting birds. That is, all the birds breeding on the island, which is flat and treeless. He had noticed that the Arctic terns, ringed plovers, lapwings and black-headed gulls had all been suffering. Far fewer young were fledging. This coincided with an increase in sightings of hedgehogs around the island, so much so that questions were asked at the island council meetings about how the hedgehogs had got to the island in the first place. 'It was all rather embarrassing,' admitted the postman, John Tulloch.

Hedgehogs have often been given a helping hand in their quest for global domination, jumping borders as accidental stowaways, or deliberately as ambassadors.

Indeed, John Tulloch was not the first to bring hedgehogs to the archipelago. They were first deliberately released on Orkney in 1870 and in the 1930s the crew from two cargo boats, the *Cormorant* and the *Busy Bee*, handed out hedgehogs to small boys playing on the pier at Kirkwall.

But in 1985 things were serious. One of the lighthouse keepers, Stuart Kirbest, described regularly seeing 'in the teens' of hedgehogs on the road each night as he returned home. Of course, Kirbest is not his real name, for there is a great shortage of surnames on North Ronaldsay – just two, in fact, Swanney and Tulloch, dominate the graveyard. People tend to refer to folk by the name of their croft. Stuart Swanney lived at Kirbest, a croft that was once the home of Ragna the Wise and her son Thorstein the Strong in the early part of the twelfth century.

Kevin thought there might be a relationship between this rapid increase in hedgehog numbers and the decline in the breeding success of his beloved birds. But to prosecute his case against the illegal aliens, he needed evidence. He needed an ecological survey, a survey that would reveal hedgehogs as little more than spiky rats with good PR. And there is no better way to get an ecological survey on the cheap than to hire an undergraduate.

He contacted his old friend Jim Fowler at Leicester Polytechnic to see if he could find help. He needed proof of the hedge-hogs' egg-eating ways. After all, this was a national emergency and the *Sunday Express* had spoken; two of Britain's best-loved forms of wildlife were up against each other and no sacrifice should be spared. Who would give up their summer holidays, wrenched from parties, lovers and friends? For better or worse, the student was me.

I remember being shown slides of the island. It looked bleak, an unwelcoming wart at the conjunction of the North Sea and the Atlantic, with uninterrupted views to the Arctic Ocean. Was going there such a good idea?

But what an opportunity. The final-year project of any degree can have a tendency to be pretty bland, being done just because it needs to be done. This was a real study. There was a need to know how many hedgehogs there were and whether they were really having such a disastrous impact on the ground-nesting birds. Now, it is not that I am unmoved by the beauty of birds. Far from it, I have spent countless hours watching them, getting absorbed in their grace and beauty. But I have always found mammals more interesting. And of the mammals, it has been the smaller ones that attracted me most. I remember as a child being taken to Skomer off the Pembrokeshire coast – an island famous for its birds. We were all asked what we wanted to see and most people were excited about puffins. I asked about small

mammals. I must have only just come across the term and was sweetly unaware that they tend to be nocturnal, or that Skomer has its own very special vole.

So I was a little conflicted. My instinct sided with the hedgehog, but my training as an ecologist weighed heavily upon me. Could I remain objective, just record the evidence before my eyes and not allow my love affair with wildlife to interfere?

A quick scan of the scientific literature made it obvious that no one had paid much attention to the problem of how to count hedgehogs. In fact, no one had paid much attention to hedgehogs. More was published on their physiology than on their behaviour and ecology.

Hedgehogs have been ignored for good reason: in recent times they have been considered neither pest, nor game, nor food. Benign species are often forgotten. But once the hunt was on to prove that hedgehogs weren't so benign, well, they began to receive a lot more attention.

And so, with this trip, came my life with hedgehogs. The stomach-churning hell I was enduring on the ferry was the beginning of a journey into a new way of seeing the world, much closer to the ground.

The series of unlooked-for steps that led me to this species has continued to this day, allowing me to develop an appreciation for the hedgehog that goes way beyond the sentimental relationship that can infect our contact with the natural world. This depth of relationship convinces me that the hedgehog has much to tell us about the way we live within what is left of the natural environment. This journey was the start of my transformation into a hedgehog advocate.

Though at the time all I could care about was getting off the bloody boat.

I was going so poorly equipped. To be honest, I had not really much of an idea about what I was going to do. Obviously I knew what a hedgehog looked like, and that there was only one species of hedgehog living wild in the UK. Heading east, there is a chance of bumping into *Erinaceus concolor*, known, unsurprisingly, as the eastern European hedgehog. Both species are about the same size, but the eastern one, found from around the Czech Republic, has a distinctive white patch of fur across its chest.

The two species evolved their distinct characteristics from a common species that bestrode the earth some 700,000 years ago. Along came ice ages that left pockets of these ancestors in the west and east of southern Europe, where, isolated and perhaps a little bored, they began to speciate, to form two individual species.

So what might happen on North Ronaldsay? Wait long enough and perhaps there will be another species. But back in 1986 the more immediate concern was whether the reports in the media of a plague of 10,000 hedgehogs were plausible. The case for the prosecution seemed to rely on this number, but it seemed unlikely that there could be so many, until I sat down with a pen and paper.

If the first couple, assuming it was a couple and not two pregnant females, had a litter of six the first year, and then assuming good survival over winter and, quite reasonably, an even gender split, that would mean four females for the next year. Each of these could have a further six – and possibly twelve if they squeezed a second litter in ... so this would mean that, with the impossible situation of 100 per cent infant survival, there would be over 9,000 hedgehogs by the end of year six. I gave up then as the numbers got too long, but there was another four years of potentially exponential growth to consider. And that was assuming John Tulloch was the only islander smuggling hedgehogs.

Luckily, exponential growth tends not to carry on forever, unlike the journey to North Ronaldsay. From Leicester to Inverness, where the train carefully did not link up with the next one, the station was cold and the toilets were locked. Then the ferry to Stromness and the bus to Kirkwall. All in all, it would have been quicker to fly to Australia. And that still left the heaving journey by ferry to my destination.

Mainland Orkney is a wonderful place, riddled with history and some of the finest whisky money can buy. Highland Park is our most northerly distillery and, like many things on the seventy or so islands, started out in a fairly disreputable way. In the 1790s a local church officer took to hiding the product of his illicit still under the pulpit of his church.

The disreputable nature of the islands extends to the land-scape. Orkney is not all flat. Hoy, for example, rears up out of the mist with the phallic greeting of the 'Old Man' as the ferry rolls by. And South Ronaldsay has sheer cliffs that have the added attraction of being home to some rather feisty 'bonxies'. The Orcadians are happy to tell it like it is. While a bird may be better known as a great skua or even *Stercorarius skua*, if it has a habit of attacking misguided human interlopers with a powerful and plummeting thump to the head, it will be called a bonxie. And then there were the 'pick a'terno', another avian menace which makes its home on North Ronaldsay and was one of the reasons for my visit. They were thought to be suffering at the rapacious jaws of the humble hedgehog.

North Ronaldsay now has a regular air service and two boats a week. But in 1986 there were far fewer flights, all beyond my budget, and just the one ferry. This was a boat that was designed to accentuate every roll, every tilt, every yaw, swell and undulation. My teeth felt sick. I sat, fixated on the horizon, sweating. My lips turned grey.

Never has the sight of land been so appreciated, though it looked as if a single sizeable wave could swallow the low-lying island whole. Kevin came to greet me with Rosie and Fly – two wonderful collies, directly related to the stray that followed Kevin home one drunken night in Manchester as he was training to be a doctor.

Kevin and the dogs took me on a tour of the island, which, as it is only 20 kilometres in circumference, was brief. He rattled off the names of places as we sped past in his bone-shaking 2CV of multiple parentage: Gravity, Muckle Gersty, Haskie Taing, Trolla Vatn, Gretchen Loch and Bride's Ness.

The beauty of the place and the names was only marred by his style of driving, which gave more attention to passing birds than the road.

That first night I decided to acclimatize myself, so, embold-ened with whisky, I headed out into the dark. The single-track road runs away from you into a slight depression. The mist clung to the ground, as if I was wading into a grey and luminous sea. It had been a really bad idea to watch the film *American Werewolf in London* just before leaving England. After a few hours of meandering, I returned rather despondently, having seen not a single hedgehog.

In retrospect, my naivety was quite sweet. I was unprepared, untrained and dropped in at the deep end. Only just before boarding the ferry to the island did it dawn on me that a pair of gloves might be useful. And I had forgotten that I would need to work out a way of weighing the hedgehogs, so busy was I with just getting there. The weight of the hedgehogs is the simplest piece of data that I could collect – along with the sex and location. Who knew, maybe it would reveal something, so I borrowed a spring balance from the bird observatory and fashioned a container out of a plastic ice-cream tub in which to place the hedgehogs.

As for counting hedgehogs, they tend to look rather alike, so I marked each one individually. A thorough review of the scientific literature revealed that the best technique was to daub spots of paint on the spines. I had come equipped with small tester pots. But the only tester pots on sale were in lighter shades of this and that – no primary colours available. Pastel it was. This is where the weight of the hedgehogs helped, I found, as the colours were not always that distinct, but referring back to weight and sex helped narrow down the options.

The marking was simple. The first received a blob of 'sea blue' on the right shoulder, top left for the second, middle for the third, etc. Then there were combinations – so hedgehog number 46 was top-right yellow and bottom-left blue (and I couldn't let the hundredth hedgehog pass without celebration. The poor female was branded with a beautiful combination of green, pink, blue and yellow). This all meant that I could identify where the hedgehogs had previously been found, keep track of their weight if they were caught more than once, and by some clever statistical manipulation hopefully calculate an estimate for the population from the proportion of animals that were recaptured. The technique is known as 'mark, release, recapture'.

My supervisor had confidently expected me to find dozens of animals every night – but he was an ornithologist, used to waiting for birds to fly into nets, not having to hunt his prey. I walked the island, spending up to six hours a night being seduced by cow pats, tussocks of grass and stones, leaping over fences to capture non-existent hedgehogs.

So pitiful was the rate of capture that I began to experiment. First I took out Tarzan. A bear of a black Labrador, this slobber monster had developed a habit of picking up hedgehogs while out for a walk. And when I took him out, he did just that. But only one of the twelve hogs he found was female. This could either indicate a very strange population dynamic on the island or be a reminder that males smell more. But I stopped using Tarzan when I began to notice the blood. Not hedgehog blood; the daft dog was so excited by this new game that he continued until his mouth was lacerated by a few too many spines.

The rate of capture was still so slow that I was willing to try anything. So after abandoning Tarzan I moved on to the idea of setting traps. There is not much of a market for hedgehog traps, so they are rather hard to come by. With the help of Kevin I set about knocking chicken wire and wooden boxes into quite the most amazing hedgehog traps the island had ever seen.

A simple one-way swing door leading to an enclosure baited with dog food, and, hey presto, we had created an utterly useless waste of time. Six traps out for fourteen days and just one hedgehog.

During midsummer there was no need for a torch, the sun dipping below the horizon for only a few minutes. And when the weather was kind, the night air was filled with the sounds of corncrakes, curlews and snipe.

There were nights when, for no discernible reason, I found not one single animal. Yet there were other nights when the place seemed to be crawling with them. And while, to begin with, I fretted about the lack of data, the more I got to know the island, the less it seemed to matter. North Ronaldsay has a magical quality and I was drawn into its idiosyncrasies.

The sheep, for example, are a raggedy bunch. The first thing you notice is that they are on the beach. This is not an accident; they live there and eat seaweed. The wall that surrounds the island is to keep them off the grass.

Each croft has an allotment of sheep, marked with specific ear cuts. But the sheep are not kept in individual herds – they roam the shoreline in delinquent gangs, only occasionally brought to book in what is possibly one of the last acts of communal farming in Britain.

My job was to stand in a line with about six other folk, holding up a fence that would gently guide the sheep into stonewalled 'punds'. Another team of people had started further around the coast and were driving the sheep towards us. Now, I have helped on farms before, I have helped with sheep before, and on the whole, when confronted with a line of people being noisy and aggressive, sheep tend to do what is required. Not this lot: like the islanders, they are a belligerent bunch of free-thinkers who paused, sized up weaknesses in the barrier and then charged straight at us, some managing to leap over by barging the human fence posts to the ground.

Their reluctance to be penned is understandable. While my dithering attempt at shearing must have been unpleasant, that is nothing to the process of castration. A small slice through the scrotum, a firm yank and the male lambs have the unenviable chance of seeing their balls thrown to the gulls.

My summer of fieldwork flew by remarkably quickly and, despite all the worry at the start, I had good data: some impor-tant and some unexpected. I was surprised by the high propor-tion of blond hedgehogs on the island; not albino, as they still had dark eyes, but around a third of the animals found had very blond spines. I still have an envelope with spines from the island and the banding that is common on most hedge-hogs is almost entirely absent on some of these. It seems that this is an island trait, as many of the hedgehogs on Alderney in the Channel Islands are also blond. And I did not find a single flea on our adven-ture. It is possible that John Tulloch de-fleaed the original two, or that they had no fleas. And as there were no hedgehogs on the island before, there were no hedgehog fleas waiting for the newcomers.

The important news came from the census. There certainly seemed to be far fewer hedgehogs on the island than the newspapers had reported. For example, Stuart, the lighthouse keeper who had previously seen in the teens of hedgehogs each night, had seen only one hedgehog while I was on the island – he felt that there had been a catastrophic decline in numbers.

But so catastrophic that, from a potential population of 10,000, I found just 138 individuals? Was I spectacularly incompetent at finding hedgehogs? Was the prosecution's case based on sound science, or was there something fishy about the figure in the first place?

Of those 138, I recaptured forty-eight. This allowed me to spend some time playing with the statistics, creatively juggling digits and revealing that it is possible to generate an answer that is clearly utter nonsense. Various techniques presented population estimates ranging from eight to 1,686. Spot the problem there? I had found 138 hedgehogs, so how could there have been only eight? Whenever you are confronted by scientists telling you something that relies on statistics, you are right to be cautious. I tried again, this time in the company of rather more expert players of the game, and came to the conclusion that, after all this, there were not 10,000 hedgehogs on the island, just 514 (plus or minus 100). This meant that I was 95 per cent certain that the number of hedgehogs on the island lay between 414 and 614. A summer's work boiled down to a few numbers.

So, a massive decrease from the 10,000 reported. But then that figure needs to be looked at a little bit closer. What was actually said, by Kevin, was the factually correct statement that he estimated the population to be between 1,000 and 10,000; because broad estimates tend to be given by 'factors'. He believed there to be over 1,000 hedgehogs but fewer than the next order of 10,000, so quite reasonably he gave both figures; and quite reasonably the journalist chose to discard the smaller number.

Knowing the number was only part of the deal. There was no doubt that some hedgehogs were eating some birds' eggs. There was no doubt that the number of hedgehogs on the island had been seen to increase at the same time as the breeding success of these birds declined. But were hedgehogs the cause? On this first visit it was impossible to say.

There was talk at the bird observatory about what was best to do – being a man of action, Kevin really felt that something needed to be done about the hedgehogs. So he suggested airlifting the beasts back to where they had come from. Obviously this was just a joke. Who would pay for it? Where would the hedgehogs go? How would the animals be captured? Kevin talked about an adoption scheme where people would offer to rehome hedgehogs. He wondered whether this would appeal to Logan Air, the local airline, as something to give them publicity. Kevin was always full of ideas and some of them were just absurd; this one obviously fell into that bracket.

So I returned to England and the process of writing up my work and completing my degree. But just a few days later everyone knew about the hedgehogs on North Ronaldsay. By a strange coincidence, Kevin's thoughts about getting people all over the UK to adopt hedgehogs from the island and an interview he did on local radio happened just as the Queen Mother, in Scotland on holiday, entered hospital for an operation. So there were TV crews hanging around waiting for something to do ... and what better way to spend the time than to descend on a small island that had cooked up a barmy idea about getting hedgehogs adopted by people all over the UK to save the birds. Kevin and the TV crews got all the islanders out searching for hedgehogs, boxing them up and loading them on to a plane. It would be hard to concoct a more perfect 'and finally' story.

The results were extraordinary. Hundreds of letters came in from all over the country, the furthest being the Isle of Wight. Logan Air stepped in, offering free flights for hedgehogs. Adopters arrived at Scottish airports and picked up their spiky cargo. TV crews came from all over the world and islanders came out in force for the cameras, searching the island for the illegal immigrants.

A Japanese journalist cornered one of the local children. The child just kept nodding and saying 'aye, aye, aye' to a stream of questions, neither party willing to admit that they could not understand a word of what was going on. There is probably an out-take TV show in Tokyo that generates many a chuckle from this clip.

In the case of hedgehogs v. birds, the prosecution pre-empted the verdict and deported the immigrants without any real evidence that they were the main problem, and without an idea of how many animals there were to start with. But its execution was a typically inspired response from Kevin.

Around 180 hedgehogs were shipped off the island over the next few years. Initially people who were adopting them arranged for transport from the mainland, but in later years hedgehogs were just dropped off on mainland Orkney to fend for themselves. Did this make a difference to the breeding success of the birds? We shall see.

Unaware of what was in store for me, I left North Ronaldsay and the hedgehogs, did an MSc, counted mice and voles for a while, went to Tanzania for three months doing conservation education work and then went to Morocco and unsurprisingly failed to find the – extinct – Barbary leopard.

But once bitten by the hedgehog bug it is hard to resist and in 1991, with the help of the Vincent Wildlife Trust, the British Hedgehog Preservation Society and the indefatigable zoologist Derek Yalden from Manchester University, I returned to the island, this time accompanied by my girlfriend.

The bird observatory was booming. Five years earlier Kevin had been pretty much alone, but now he had a team of volunteers working to create one of the most important birding centres in the country. And his environmental plans were also coming on apace. He had persuaded a university to run a wind-energy project at the observatory, giving him a turbine.

I got to know that turbine pretty well, as we pitched our tent beneath it. There is no mistaking the fact that wind turbines are noisy. But having spent three months sleeping beneath one, I can attest that they are nowhere near as noisy as a flysheet in the wind. And outside it was no more than the noise of trees.

On my first visit I had been an unwitting pawn; this time I wanted to set my own agenda and, while not acting directly for the defence, I wanted at least to ensure that the hedgehogs got a fair hearing. I wanted to see how many hedgehogs there were. Had the airlift made an impact? And I wanted to see what other threats the birds were facing. Were hedgehogs the only culprit?

Hedgehogs, and most mammals in fact, were still treated with disdain. The observatory was utterly split on taxonomic lines, with the obsessive birders condescending to allow mere mammal enthusiasts to share their table, though we did have to sleep outside.

The more time I spent with them, the more I realized that for some, at least, this was little more than glorified trainspotting, meeting a need to collect and catalogue. Obviously counting hedgehogs is an entirely more reasonable enterprise.

Sometimes it felt rather like it was us against the ornithologists. And as my companion began to be seduced (not just by birds) it was very much me against the hedgehog-hating world.

I am pretty open-minded, happy to spend time with birds as well as mammals. So I made a concerted effort to see what pressures the birds were under, and focused on the Arctic tern. This slight, angelic-looking bird is a wonder of the world. Emerging from an egg on North Ronaldsay, it grows up rapidly in preparation for the longest migration of any species. As our days begin to shorten it heads south; not south as in Costa del Sol south, but really south. Arctic terns can do a round trip of 35,000 kilometres, all the way down to the Antarctic and back again.

As beautiful and amazing as this animal is, there are considerable disadvantages in choosing it for a species to study. This was rammed home with some vigour when I accompanied people from the observatory as we headed out along a stretch of shingle, trying to find tern nests with chicks. The plan was to put a small ring on the leg of each chick found – part of the international effort to track birds.

The first to suffer had the disadvantage of being, as he put it, '5 foot 20' (fed up of being asked just how tall he was). Blood trickled down his face from the wound on his scalp caused by the beak of a very angry tern. Another assistant warden took heed and placed his tobacco tin under his rarely removed woolly hat. The work was punctuated by occasional sounds of beak on tin as his protection proved its worth. I tried to stay close to the tall guy.

The hours I spent sitting at the margins of a tern colony monitoring the amount of food being brought in to the chicks were some of the most nerve-jangling of my life. Measuring the amount of food required that I assess the size of the sand eels carried in by the parents. These small fish are a staple of much marine life – fulmars, kittiwakes and guillemots depend on them. Watching each delivery through binoculars, I had to compare the length of the sand eel with the length of beak – a very simple yet effective tool.

Common terns also visit the island and it still tickles me that if birders are not sure if they have seen a common or an Arctic tern, the accepted shorthand is 'comic'.

My Arctic terns did not have it all their own way on the persecution stakes. As they tried to deliver their cargo of fish to their chicks, they would frequently come under attack from Arctic skuas loitering around the edge of the colony. These agile birds are well named in Latin, *Stercorarius parasiticus*; they are kleptoparasites. They steal fish from smaller birds by chasing them until they drop their hard-won cargo.

And hedgehog hunters don't have it all their own way either – similar kleptoparasitism was in evidence at the bird observatory as one of the wardens swooped in on my girlfriend. I emptied a vomiting fulmar over him in a show of impotent petulance. His clothes will have stunk for weeks. Made me feel better.

Nights out with the hedgehogs were sometimes magical and sometimes farcical. The sublime was offered by shooting stars and the northern lights; the ridiculous came from the interruption by a wire fence to an enthusiastic dash by my soon-to-be ex. Face down in a field of cow dung. Made me feel better.

Reprieve came in the form of the summer dance, a very pagan event where islanders celebrate life by trying to drink themselves to death – a ceilidh like no other.

Two Olympians pulled me into the mêlée for the 'Dashing White Sergeant': two women leading one clueless man. This was not a sensual and provocative dance; this was a failed attempt at maintaining my dignity. Alcohol was absorbed in the traditional banana sandwich break, followed by more alcohol as islanders toasted their Viking heritage and the small band of accordion, fiddle and drums started up again.

Unable to compete in the grand excess of drinking and already rather bruised from the eightsome reel, I wandered outside into the perpetual twilight of Orkney summer – cooling, fresh and pleasantly lonely – and there was a hedgehog, reminding me that it was still office hours.

I was keeping a record of the weights of the hedgehogs because, in the first study, it looked like these island hogs were on the large side. And again, the data were clear: males averaged 971g, females 828g, around 30 per cent heavier than their mainland relatives. This could be because the two original imports were on the robust side of average, or it could just have been all those birds' eggs. The data also revealed an unexpected difference between the sexes. On the mainland hedgehogs usually weigh 600–700 grams, with little difference between male and female.

Whatever their size, something I have grown to realize is that hedgehogs are more often heard than seen. Certainly at home in Oxford I am much more likely to hear the distinctive snuffling as they trundle through the undergrowth. But on North Ronaldsay the almost constant wind made this much less likely. There was one behaviour, however, that I would invariably hear before I saw – and this is a behaviour that regularly gets hedgehogs into the newspapers: courtship.

Hedgehog courtship is an understandably cautious process, for the male in particular. This is a species where no really does mean no.

Females can be fertile any time from when they emerge from hibernation in April until they begin to get ready for it again in September, though the main period for courtship is May and June.

When a male comes across a female that is exhibiting some evidence of being fertile – that is, she smells just right – he will begin to make advances. More often than not, judging by the times I have witnessed the behaviour, the female rebuffs him with a small jump forward and a sneeze-like plosive. This is the strange huffing and puffing that many a householder has been disturbed by at night, frequently resulting in letters to the papers, or calls to the police. As happened in Bremen, Germany, when a couple were disturbed by strange noises. The police arrived and shone torches, finding two hedgehogs described unusually eloquently by the police spokesman as being 'loudly engaged in ensuring the continuity of their species'.

The fear that this noise can engender should not be sneezed at. I got a letter from a Caroline Sykes recently in which she describes vividly the horror of being in a very quiet caravan park in Worcestershire with her four daughters and hearing what conjured up for her a 'sexual pervert' and then 'a deer impaled on the fence gasping its last agonized breaths'. Almost hysterical with fear, she ran to the warden's chalet. He emerged, listened to the story, got a shovel and strode out in silence. He scooped under the caravan and sent something flying into the woodland nearby. 'Hedgehogs,' is all he said as he stomped back to bed.

This is not the only noise a hedgehog makes. One hedgehog rescuer in Twickenham, Greater London, related a wince-inducing tale. She had just been handed a bundle of four baby hedgehogs from a disturbed nest. No mother to be seen; yet they stood a good chance of survival in her capable hands. She went to make up some more formula milk to give them a feed when the air was split with a terrifying screech. She dropped everything and ran to find one of the babies screaming in agony, as one of the others frantically suckled at the closest thing she could find to a teat: his penis.

A courting male continues his noisy pursuit of the female, trying to get around to her rear; she continues to turn with obstructive obstinacy. This merry dance can continue for hours – well, not so merry really; it does look rather grumpy. But the circling continues and sometimes, if they are performing in long grass, or even a crop field, there results a small arena of flattened stems, all pointing in the same direction as if layered by supernatural forces. It was this phenomenon that led to my favourite newspaper headline of all time: 'Hedgehogs cleared of corn circle dementia'.

The headline also hinted at a mysterious hedgehog behaviour, one so rare that I can only report on other people's sightings. Why do some hedgehogs sometimes run manically in circles for hours, pivoting around nothing discernable to the human eye?

All that courtship inevitably generates babies. When I found my first juvenile, a pretty little thing the size of my fist, I very quickly remembered what I had been taught five years earlier on my first visit. They may seem small and defenceless, but juvenile hedgehogs have a very effective trick up their sleeves:

their new-found spines. And let me tell you, those spines, unblunted by use, are very sharp. Plus a defensive move that is exquisite in its timing: as my bare fingers touched the back of the hoglet, it made a noise like a sneeze and jumped. Now, imagine that is the nose of an inquisitive dog? Quite an effective repellent. So, treat those youngsters with respect.

The fact that there were youngsters indicated that the North Ronaldsay population was still active, but had it managed to maintain the levels that generated such news a few years before? Well, the population had undoubtedly fallen dramatically. Using the same technique as last time, I estimated the total population to be around 105 – I found and marked a total of seventy hedgehogs and had fifty-seven recaptures. An indication that I was getting close to marking most of the population was that, in the last three weeks, of the thirty-five hedgehogs I found, only three were new.

People on the island expressed surprise that there were even this many; in the intervening five years they had drifted out of sight and out of mind. So why were the populations of ground-nesting birds showing no concomitant recovery? Because ecology is never as simple as people would like it to be. The study of individual populations of animals and plants is hard enough, and these populations are never in isolation.

I found evidence that hedgehogs ate the eggs of Arctic terns by feeding quail eggs (a similar size) to hedgehogs – they leave a distinctive pattern in the shell, a small rectangle with the gap between the upper front teeth of the hog being revealed by an uneven entry point. The hedgehog would have then used its tongue to lap up the rich contents. I found tern eggs with the same pattern of damage. This was very different from bird damage, which was either a crush from both sides by a bigger bird, or a stab from one of the smaller ones. I also found the remains of black-headed gull chicks left over by a hedgehog (nothing else would have stayed in the raucous colony to consume the hatchling), though these were probably eaten as carrion.

Was there enough evidence to support the prosecution's case? The prosecution still maintained that hedgehogs were to blame for the decline in bird breeding success, but my survey of sand eels showed that the amount of food the chicks were getting was far lower than in similar studies in other places. Were the tern chicks starving? Was this because of overfishing of sand eels? The small fish are hoovered from the ocean to be minced and processed into feed for caged fish and pigs. The annual quotas for the sand eel, a species that can make up to 50 per cent of all the fish in the North Sea, are not being met simply because the factory ships cannot find them. For example, in one year the Danish fleet caught only 300,000 tonnes of its

950,000-tonne quota. And the fishing industry complains when the scientists suggest a cut in quotas?

Other theories include evidence that climate change is forcing the plankton on which the sand eels feed to move further north, forcing terns to fly further to find food for their chicks on North Ronaldsay. Or that the warmer surface waters are forcing the sand eels to live deeper, out of reach of the plunging terns.

There were many other impacts on the terns: oystercatchers, starlings and turnstones are all known to take their eggs; cats were seen prowling and vehicles had driven through colonies. Perhaps the black-headed gulls also gave a clue. I visited a large colony on the edge of Hooking Loch, deep in a field of yellow flag irises, helping the birders ring the young. We found about fifty chicks, despite the clamour of angry parents. On a return visit nine days later there was a very different sight: hardly a single live chick was to be found. They were just dead on their nests. If a predator had caused this, then the bodies would have been eaten, and if it was starvation, where there were two chicks, one would have died first. But these all looked to have died at the same time. Had the colony been ravaged by an outbreak of disease? Or perhaps the chicks had been deserted due to the disturbance caused by the invasion of ornithologists.

Whatever the cause of the terns' failure to breed, it has had a tragic effect. In 2005 Kevin described a 'silent spring', as the shrill terns just gave up and left. They have been back each year since, but the chicks that hatch rarely make it to fledging.

The impact of this absence of young is felt by more than just the terns. As Kevin explained, 'The skuas that used to harass the terns have turned their attention to wader chicks, so there is now a decline in their breeding success as well. The natural system has been knocked out of kilter.'

And there rests the case for the defence. There have been no sightings of hedgehogs on the island for five years, yet the Arctic tern population has not recovered. Was there ever a relationship?

There is a tendency for wildlife management to elicit an uncontrolled jerking of the knee, with the blame landing on the latest or most obvious incomer. While in the case of North Ronaldsay, this seems to have been unjustified, that does not mean hedgehogs are perfect. Sometimes they really are the bad guys.

New Zealand

In retrospect it was utterly crazy, but as the colonialists moved in on the Land of the Long White Cloud, so they sought to make it a little more like home. They needed help acclimatizing to this distant paradise. So they set up the Acclimatization Society – one of many that were set up around the world. Not content with wreaking havoc among the human inhabitants, the colonists also sought to screw up the ecosystem as well.

Maybe I am being unfair. It is only with the gift of hindsight that we can see the dangerously short-sighted nature of passing legislation to encourage the introduction of alien species that would 'contribute to the pleasure and profit of the inhabitants'. The 1861 Animal Acclimatization Act still has an impact today as conservationists struggle to contain the damage caused by the deliberate and accidental releases: deer, ferrets, goats, pigs, rabbits, rats, stoats, weasels and, of course, hedgehogs have all helped to change the environment.

You can understand why deer and rabbits would be introduced – food, aesthetics, sport – they were utilitarian choices. But why hedgehogs – nocturnal, secretive and not much fun to hunt? And their introduction was no accident. Hedgehogs were a very deliberate introduction. It has all been documented by ecologist Robert Brockie. He has rummaged through the original documentation and charted the official progress of the prickly immigrants.

A pair was received by the Acclimatization Society in 1869; twenty-four hedgehogs were sent in 1871, but only one survived the journey; in 1885, 100 were sent, but only three survived and were released into a Dunedin garden; twelve more were sent in 1892 in exchange for twelve wekas, a flightless bird related to moorhens and coots.

Numbers gradually increased in the Dunedin and Christchurch areas until they were described as 'extraordinarily abundant' in 1916.

And now? Well, for good or ill, hedgehogs are an established component of New Zealand's ecosystem. There is, unsurprisingly, a divergence of views as to the merits of these upstarts. On the one hand there is the undeniable charm of the critters. People like to see them around, and for a long time they have been regarded as perhaps the most benign of the introductions. Even if they have wonky teeth. It seems that the founding fathers (or possibly mothers) of the hedgehog community had a ropey gene that has led to around half of them having missing or abnormal teeth.

Now, however, there are conservationists doing their best to rid parts of New Zealand of these malignant incomers. You see, our dearly beloved friends have a taste for many New Zealand delicacies. And New Zealand is rightly protective of its home-grown beasts. There have been hedgehogs found with rare native beetle remains in their stomachs, including one containing 283 weta legs. Now, I have seen pictures of weta – an amazingly large cricket – and this is testament to the voracity of the hedgehog's appetite. They are scary-looking bugs.

Auckland Regional Pest Management Strategy has the hedgehog on its hit list. But there is no plan for a blanket eradication. New Zealand's conservationists are working on the principle that it is better to protect pockets of what is very special than to try to defend the entire country from a mass of invaders – of which hedgehogs are one of the most benign.

Not everyone in New Zealand has such animosity towards the hedgehogs. Certainly the world would be a poorer place if it were not for Burton Silver's Bogor cartoons – featuring the eponymous hero, a lone woodsman, who shares a very funny world with a population of snail and marijuana-munching hedgehogs. There is also a chain of bike shops throughout the country called Hedgehog Bikes. And an attempt was made by McGillicuddy's Serious Party to get a hedgehog elected to Parliament.

New Zealand is not alone in trying to catch the hedgehog vote. Stuart Hughes stood in Devon in 1991 for the Raving Loony Green Giant Party and one of his key manifesto proposals called for the lowering of the buttons at pedestrian crossings to enable hedgehogs to cross safely. I would have voted for him.

Brockie has been keeping an eye on New Zealand's hedgehogs since the 1950s and has noticed that, rather than sweeping the islands, they have suffered a substantial fall in numbers:

> Hedgehog numbers peaked in the 1960s, when I was seeing 40–50 hedgehog corpses per 100 kilometres of road. Now that figure is down to just 1 per 100 kilometres, pretty much the same as in Britain. Nevertheless zealots are killing them here in the sand dunes because they classify them in with rats, stoats and ferrets – the real culprits in the destruction of native fauna.

And not just killing them. Leaping, rather unfortunately, on to the hedgehogs-as-pets bandwagon, in 1994 someone organized 120 hedgehogs to be flown from Rotorua to Miami, where they were refused entry as they had not been checked for TB and were returned. This would have presented a great solution to those in New Zealand trying to rid the islands of the pesky immigrants, but resulted in 120 hedgehogs clocking up so many 'air miles' that next time they could afford to go first class.

The Uists

'Who let the hogs out?' – *Sun*

At around the same time John Tulloch had been delivering hedgehogs to North Ronaldsay, someone, and as the story unfolds their desire for anonymity will become understandable, repeated the experiment on South Uist in the Outer Hebrides. This delivery had far more dramatic consequences; it gave headline writers a chance to exercise their wit and it also persuaded me to dust off my head torch, get out my thermal underwear and re-enter the hedgehog fray two decades later.

Ornithologist Digger Jackson had been busy counting birds out on the Uists. His work on these three islands began in the 1980s but did not really have an impact until he published a scientific paper in 2000, 'The Importance of the Introduced Hedgehog as a Predator of the Eggs of Waders on Machair in South Uist, Scotland'.

The machair, a rare, sandy habitat, is protected under European law, and the protection extends to the internationally important populations of dunlins and ringed plovers that breed there each spring – around the same time some 7,000 hedgehogs emerge, hungry, from hibernation.

The legislation required that the relevant authority, Scottish Natural Heritage, take action to protect the eggs of the birds and in 2001 they commissioned a report from hedgehog expert Nigel Reeve.

There were three options once you accepted that the status

quo was untenable: remove the hedgehogs, fence the nesting birds, or a combination of the two. The real question became that of how to remove the hedgehogs? Dead or alive?

'Slaughter of the innocents is a prickly subject'
— *Press and Journal*, Scottish newspaper

In 2003, hedgehogs hit the headlines: Scottish Natural Heritage had decided that hedgehogs must be killed. As the newspapers filled with the story of the forthcoming cull, I assumed that Nigel Reeve must have uncovered something new in his research. The reasons given by SNH for the decision to kill hedgehogs was that moving them would be cruel, that the translocated hedgehogs would suffer a 'slow and lingering death', that they would succumb to unnamed diseases or oust resident hedgehogs. Which was all news to me: my experience with hedgehogs in Devon certainly suggested that far less well-equipped hedgehogs fare well on release into a new environment.

I decided I wanted to see the situation on the Uists for myself and managed to persuade the BBC's Natural History Unit to lend me the kit to record a piece about the cull for radio. I went, perhaps surprisingly for someone with such a professed love of hedgehogs, with a rather ambivalent attitude to their fate — I really respect Nigel Reeve and if he had said they must die, then, sadly, I would agree.

The public face of the cull was SNH's George Anderson. He was adamant. Killing hedgehogs was the only way — and he even made a counterintuitive case on the grounds of hedgehog welfare. Killing them was less stressful than keeping them caged for a week on the island, surrounded by other hedgehogs – these are solitary animals. And then there is the transporting to the mainland (do hedgehogs get seasick?), being housed in a new rescue centre before being released into an unfamiliar garden. He could be right, I suppose; perhaps a quick death was better. But something felt wrong with the argument.

The RSPCA, their Scottish counterparts the SSPCA, and hundreds of other carers rescue, look after and release thousands of hedgehogs into unfamiliar places each year. Is all this work for naught?

'Mrs Tiggywinkle brigade can't halt a prickly pogrom' – *Daily Mail*

I finished my interview with George Anderson still feeling something was not right and went off in search of the other side of the debate. Because this is what made the story all the more fascinating: not only was there a cull of hedgehogs, but there was also a team of people on the islands doing their darnedest to save as many hedgehogs as possible from lethal injection.

Uist Hedgehog Rescue was a coalition of Advocates for Animals, the British Hedgehog Preservation Society (BHPS), International Animal Rescue and the Hessilhead Wildlife Rescue Trust, for the first year also joined by the Wildlife Hospital Trust from St Tiggywinkles. They had set up a rescue centre on Benbecula, lying in between North and South Uist; causeways connect them.

UHR spokesperson Ross Minett added a well-needed touch of glamour to the proceedings (he was recently voted Europe's sexiest vegetarian). He explained how the conflict started. I was shocked to find that Nigel's original study, which had actually looked at the feasibility of translocating hedgehogs alive, had been dismissed, with SNH contracting John Kirkwood, director of the Humane Slaughter Association, to produce a further report. Do you think he might be coming to the table with a little bit of baggage? What did he decide was the most humane solution? Slaughter, obviously.

He concluded that the welfare implications of translocating hedgehogs were just too great. He dismissed contraception, as the technology has yet to be developed. Rather bizarrely, he investigated the idea of a hedgehog zoo to house them, a sort of Guantanamo Bay, illegal combatants from the war on egg-eaters. In the end he went with what he knew best.

And then came the personal shock: evidence that Kirkwood used to justify his position was from some of my own work – a rather inappropriate extrapolation I believe, as the situations were far removed. My work had been looking at the survival of overwintered juveniles being released after six months of captivity, not healthy adults being held for a week or so.

To try to prevent the cull, UHR and the Mammals Trust (UK) tried to develop a study that would satisfy SNH's concerns about hedgehog welfare. Pat Morris was heavily involved and when I asked him about it he became uncharacteristically explicit. 'SNH has been obdurate in its communications with the people who know about hedgehog ecology and hedgehog welfare,' he said. 'At short notice, SNH requested a scientific study to prove that no significant damage was done to trans-located Uist animals or the recipient population. The latter is impossible to prove. Our workable proposal for a study was then rejected by SNH leaving too little time to set up a study for this season. SNH knew that at the time. Their objections to the proposal were unrealistic.'

Pat also explained that some of the science SNH was quoting was wrong. The claim was made that if hedgehogs were moved from the Uists to the mainland, the mainland population would suffer because of additional competition for resources. Sort of a 'one in, one out' policy – you add a hedgehog to the popula-tion near Glasgow and another one falls off Beachy Head. This is known as 'density dependent' population regulation.

But that is not how it works with hedgehogs. The controlling factor of hedgehog population size is not density. Overwinter survival is probably a more important mechanism. And it is also worth considering that whatever natural mechanism has evolved over the last 20 million years to govern hedgehog numbers, there is the very new 'predation' from cars to consider. A few more from the Western Isles are really not going to tip the balance.

It also became clear, from talking to hedgehog carers, that there were no diseases that the hedgehogs were likely to catch which they couldn't already find in the Outer Hebrides. It is not as if this was a population long isolated and in the process of forming a new species. And as for the fleas, again there was no evidence that a Uist hedgchog was going to suffer anything other than the odd itch should fleas take advantage of the new blood.

It felt as if SNH had decided that culling was the only option and did not want to give any ground, even in the face of very persuasive arguments from some of the most experienced hedgehog experts.

'Uist goes to war over hedgehogs galore' – *Sunday Times*

I was not the only reporter on the islands for the cull; the story had made such an impact that there was a rather impressive turn-out from the national media. Did the cull really begin on 1 April? We had been directed to assemble near a hotel before heading out into the dark to meet the team of cullers; or rather, to not meet them, but to see their silhouettes. There was a ripple of shock when SNH's spin doctor told us that we would not be able to see the faces of the people doing the cull, or learn their names, because they were in fear of the animal rights extremists who had come over to the island. Most of the journalists scribbled notes, the photographers muttered rudely under their breath about the limitations they were being confronted with, and we tried to scrabble some sort of image out of torchlight and shadowy hedgehog hunters. The media had all left the island the following morning, without the opportunity to check with the hedgehog rescuers to see if they really were animal rights extremists.

Now, I have met dangerous animal rights extremists. I was caught up in a ferocious battle at Hillgrove cat farm in Oxfordshire. As I tried to record some material about the campaign to close this breeding centre that supplied animal-testing laboratories, the mob bombarded police and the farm with a rain of stones. It was scary, though on that day the police were marginally scarier.

The folk of UHR were not like this. The most extreme thing they did was mount the first ever demonstration of its kind on the islands, standing before the shed where the killing was to take place with a banner reading 'Fly home the hedgehogs, save the waders'.

A few years later I met an animal rights activist who had gone up to the Uists the following year. A small crowd had been attracted by the publicity generated during the first year's conflict and headed up in a minibus to join all the others, who were not there, as they had never existed. The group was also rather disappointed by the lack of hedgehogs.

He explained that rather than be on the islands for a fight, they were there to save hedgehogs, so there was a mutually agreed policy that the rescuers and cullers would operate in different areas, avoiding conflict. Hedgehogs avoid conflict with mutual avoidance too.

But the animal rights lot got bored. They were finding so few hedgehogs that it was hardly worth their while staying, so they turned their attention to the sheep – another imported animal that was in need of rescuing, so they argued. They set about trying to ship a few back to the mainland and free them from a fate of cutlets and chops. I got the impression that the authorities were not too happy about the emergence of ethical sheep rustling.

SNH shot themselves in the foot a bit with this.

Not only did the painting of gentle hedgehog rescuers with a militant tag attract what they most feared, but it also meant that they were unable to change their mind. SNH could not be seen to be forced into a change of policy by the actions of a group of animal rights activists.

Bringing animal rights into the question got me thinking. It felt as if this debate had caused a shift in conventional positions. SNH had taken on the mantle of the arbiter of animal welfare, certainly not their normal job. But then serious zoologists had taken a stance based on animal rights. There was no doubting that the hedgehogs' welfare would be least affected by a swift death. But what about their right to life? Unusual to think of respectable academics donning balaclavas, but then again, perhaps we jump too quickly to conclusions when animal rights are mentioned.

'Right, lads, that's one down, just 4,999 to go' – *Daily Mail*

How do you go about rescuing hedgehogs? How could a rag-tag bunch of volunteers compete with the well-funded operation of SNH?

The carefully choreographed dance, avoiding conflict, rather put paid to the image of a scrum of people diving for hedgehogs; whoever got it determined its fate.

That said, to begin with it was hardly a level playing field. While the cullers were out at night with torches that burned the back of your eyes and left the air sizzling, the rescuers had come across a problem.

There is a practice known as 'lamping' where people go out at night, dazzle wildlife with a strong torch and, while the deer, rabbit or fox is trying to work out what the hell is going on, they get blasted with a gun. In the Wildlife and Countryside Act (1981), section 11.2.c, there are controls that require people out at night using a torch to find mammals to have a licence. So hedgehog rescuers had to have a licence. But who held the right to grant the licence? That's right, SNH. And they wouldn't.

Fortunately, there was a way around this. It was perfectly reasonable for someone to use a torch to light their path if they were out at night. After all, with those rabbit holes the machair is a potential death trap. And if, as they walk, their companion spies a hedgehog in the light of the torch, they are allowed to pick it up without a licence.

However, it quickly became apparent that wandering around at night hoping to find hedgehogs is a pretty inefficient way of going about hedgehog rescuing. So the rescuers started a bounty scheme that helped foster their place in the community. In the first year it was £5 per happy hedgehog, but this was raised to £20 the following year. The scheme was only open to islanders who had undertaken training in how to look after hogs and minimize any distress. The press, obviously, loved this idea. And some islanders made a pretty packet during the hedgehog season, which ended early enough in the

 year so as not to risk picking up nursing mothers and potentially starve their young. A gamekeeper from North Uist rescued over fifty hedgehogs and another islander netted around thirty. In total nearly £5,000 was paid in bounties to islanders – equivalent to the cost to the taxpayer of SNH killing nearly five hedgehogs.

'Duchess offers to save hedgehogs' – *The Times*

The mutual avoidance on the ground was not so evident back on the mainland and quite a war was waged through the pages of the press.

SNH spread a story that islanders were going to be the focus of attention of the tax office for not declaring the gifts they were receiving for rescuing hedgehogs (this turned out not to be the case) and the rescuers began to recruit an array of celebrities to help the cause. And what a mixed bunch. Support came in from Paul McCartney, Sting, Joanna Lumley, Richard Adams, Carla Lane, Martin Shaw and Twiggy. The Duchess of Hamilton and Tim Rice both offered their land as release sites.

A raffle to help raise funds included gifts of signed books from Ann Widdecombe and a boxload of goodies from Brian May. This was my first brush with Ann Widdecombe, MP for Maidstone and the Weald, since she had involuntarily helped me earn much needed money by being custard-pied in front of my camera. A few years later, on her sixtieth birthday, she asked her friends to make donations to the British Hedgehog Preservation Society in lieu of presents. When I met her some time later at her Whitehall office she was amazingly charming and full of love for our mutual friend.

Her love for hedgehogs came from her father and she would enjoy watching them visit their garden when she was a child. When he died, she arranged for the collection at his memorial to be for hedgehogs, and the same with her mother. So when it came to Ann's birthday there was a logical solution to a major problem. 'What I absolutely dreaded, having been through this for my fiftieth,' she explained, 'was a house full of presents for which I simply did not have room.'

I asked why she had become involved with the Uist story and she was unsurprisingly forthright. 'I saw no reason to carry out mass murder of a perfectly ordinary and inoffensive colony of hedgehogs.'

I was more surprised by the support of Brian May. My school-days had been spent dreaming of being able to play the guitar like him. I could rhapsodize about his skill; in fact, we spent an age trying to come up with suitable puns for a press release to announce his support – 'Another one spikes the dust', 'Crazy prickle thing called love', 'Culler Queen' – and got nowhere close to anything that was not awful. And however much I tried to coerce Fay at the BHPS into fixing the raffle draw, she would not let me win his contribution of musical para-phernalia. Most unfair.

I really wanted to know why he was involved, though. It seemed such an unlikely cause to champion. It is not as if he is without extracurricular activities: he has just completed his PhD in astrophysics (put on hold in 1970, when Queen took over his life) and written a modest little book about the origins of everything called *Bang: The Complete History of the Universe* and played 'God Save the Queen' on his guitar atop Buckingham Palace to celebrate the golden jubilee.

So I wrote to him, totally expecting to be fobbed off by a multi-layered bureaucracy of minders, and was delighted to get an immediate response, full of outrage. 'I was outraged when I heard of the senseless killing of healthy, native creatures ... already captive and perfectly able to be relocated,' he wrote. 'I was also outraged at the logical absurdity of a bunch of birds of very small brains being put above these delightful and intelligent mammals.'

How my heart soared when I read that – he was the first person I have come across to articulate this bird/mammal debate so simply. And to ask a very pertinent question: why do we favour some species over others? Has conservation descended to a popularity contest?

And then he raised a very interesting point. 'Most of all,' he continued, 'I was outraged that this cruelty was being defended by ... people supposedly engaged in the prevention of cruelty to animals.'

Where was the SSPCA in all of this? The Scottish Society for the Prevention of Cruelty to Animals was being remarkably quiet. The RSPCA had already said that it was 'disappointed by the decision taken by Scottish Natural Heritage to proceed with a cull of hedgehogs ...'

Strangely, the SSPCA had based their tacit support for the cull on the information supplied to them by SNH – that a translocation would lead to significant mortality. But the translocation would be doing nothing more complicated than what the SSPCA already do for hundreds of hedgehogs each year from their own Middlebank Wildlife Centre. This meant that either the SSPCA believed they themselves were releasing hedgehogs that were going to suffer a significant mortality, or they did not really believe what SNH were saying. Neither way looked good.

After the first year the tally was 150 rescued, sixty-six killed, though to be honest the figures are not entirely fair. A great deal of the effort of the cullers was applied to the island of North Uist, where there were the fewest hedgehogs. Their plan, and there is no denying its logic, was to work down the island chain, clearing all before them. I am sure there was a 'situation room' somewhere with a large map and pieces, representing hedgehogs, birds, cullers and rescuers, being pushed around by uniformed women in A-line skirts and sensible shoes, while the top brass of SNH looked down, twiddling their moustaches. Yet despite the skirts and moustaches, by 2006, after four years of culling, the rescuers were beating the killers by 756 to 658.

Killing hedgehogs is not cheap. At first glance it might seem logical that culling would be cheaper. There is none of the expense of transporting and housing the hedgehogs. But the reality was very different. In the first year SNH spent £90,000 on the Uist Wader Project – and all that money went on the programme to eradicate hedgehogs. They killed sixty-six, so that works out at £1,363 per hedgehog.

 Now, over the next three years they did get better at catching hedgehogs, but still the average cost for killing each one hog was around £1,000.

Of course, I am not being entirely fair with this calculation. The rescuers were volunteers, working for expenses only. And even when they were paying £20 to locals for each hedgehog brought in, the total cost was only around £50 to get hogs from the islands to release points on the mainland.

But the money to kill the hedgehogs was from the taxpayer, taken without consent to do something that many people objected to. The money to rescue them was voluntary contributions to a charity.

One very crucial question seemed to have been ignored, something so crucial that it amazed me. A publicly funded body could get away with spending hundreds of thousands of pounds without seeming to address it. Would the project work? Would SNH be able to kill all the hedgehogs on the Uists and, if they could eradicate the hogs, would that ensure the birds' survival?

I received assurances from the SNH spokesman that their aim was to completely remove hedgehogs from the Uists. How feasible would that be?

The only way to work that out is through 'modelling'. This is a mathematical exercise where you first of all make assumptions, based on information already collected, and then make a series of logical predictions to look at what might happen when different scenarios are played out. In this way you can work out whether it is actually possible to achieve the desired outcome.

But SNH had no modelling data to show how they expected to achieve the eradication of hedgehogs. So some researchers from the

University of London decided to have a go themselves, and came to the disturbing conclusion that if 712 hedgehogs were removed every year, the population of hedgehogs would be maintained in a steady state.

In the four years from 2003 to 2006, SNH managed to kill a total of 658 hedgehogs. So that means despite over £500,000 being spent, the number of hedgehogs on the islands might have actually increased. Combining the cull with the rescue makes it look a little more respectable, as 756 hogs were trans-located, but still that is well below the sort of level required to achieve eradication.

This is not to say that eradicating a species is not possible. The campaign against the coypu in East Anglia was successful. After escaping from fur farms in the 1930s, these large South American aquatic rodents made themselves at home in the British countryside, undermining the river banks and dykes with substantial burrows. Eradication began in 1964 and the last one was seen in December 1989. But coypu were undeni-ably alien, while hedgehogs are just slowcoaches.

To try to increase their hit rate, SNH announced that they were going to use a new tool: dogs. As I found in North Ronaldsay, dogs can be very effective at finding hedgehogs – and I was just using an enthusiastic amateur. But there are professionals out there with noses that can be fine-tuned to detect a hedgehog at a hundred paces.

So where is the problem with that? Find the hedgehog with a dog – it does not touch them, just points. Then take it off for its little injection.

Oh, but the clever people at Uist Hedgehog Rescue spotted something. The change in the law that prevented hunting with hounds also meant that if a mammal was found with a dog, it would have to be either flushed to a bird of prey or shot. Now, hedgehogs don't flush very well, as any plumber will tell you, and there are few birds of prey capable of tackling one – though eagle owls can take them. That leaves shooting, there in the field. What a PR problem – at least a lethal injection was discreet, but shooting would leave patches of bloody prickles as very clear markers around the islands. Unsurprisingly, when they realized that they could not change the law just to suit themselves, SNH gave up this unpalatable option. However, in terms of the welfare of the hedgehog, something that SNH professed to be so concerned about, a shotgun to the head is the simplest mode of execution, with no time for the animal to become stressed. They might not like it, thanks to the bad publicity, but it would be better for the hedgehog.

One of the problems we faced was that SNH continued to maintain that translocated hedgehogs would suffer. And while we were confident that previous research showed they would be fine, this was dented by an unexpected broadside from Professor Stephen Harris of Bristol University. I had long been an admirer of his work on mammals, and he was rightly considered to be an important researcher in his field. But then came this call – he was furious. He wanted to know why the BHPS had refused to fund a study of his that showed a very high mortality of rescued Uist hogs.

I immediately got in touch with the society. The answer to his question was quite simple. He had been refused funding because his study was too small to meet the needs of SNH. So even if it had been 100 per cent successful, it would have made no difference to their position.

But he left me with a niggling worry: perhaps there was something about the Uist hedgehogs that made them prone to a rapid demise on the mainland.

So in 2005 I suggested that we undertake (have you noticed the change from 'they' to 'we'? I had been recruited on to the board of the BHPS) our own study. Not one that would meet the needs of SNH, but something simple to see if rescued hedgehogs really did just curl up and die.

We only had a small budget, but I managed to find an experienced radio tracker, a release site and some pretty amazing accommodation. In fact, I was rather jealous. My accommodation while previously hedgehogging has been rather basic: a tent or a draughty and damp caravan. But I managed to secure my tracker a heated cottage right in North Ayrshire's Eglinton Country Park, where she would be working. It had everything you could dream of; it was dry, warm and had a bath. I had also found a recent graduate, Douglas Walker, who was willing to work as an assistant for expenses to gain experience in the field.

What could go wrong?

The radio tags were ordered and I found I could borrow the receivers I had used in Devon ten years before – they were rather doddery, but just about up to the task.

And then the bombshell: my tracker ran off to something more exciting. What could be more exciting than a month in early spring in the wild wasteland of North Ayrshire with the expectation of persistent rain penetrating your soul? A tropical beach counting turtles probably – the lightweight.

There are not many people qualified to do this sort of work and finding a replacement at short notice was going to be tough. My wife pointed out that I was perfect for the job. After getting clearance from the Charity Commission that being a BHPS trustee didn't interfere with me doing the work, I rewaxed my Barbour and prepared for a return to the field.

Having dumped my stuff at the comfortable cottage (I would have felt rather guilty if I had set this up for my own benefit), I headed off to Hessilhead Rescue Centre to meet my new friends and attach the little radio transmitters that would allow me to pry into their lives at least once a night.

The next morning was my one chance to get a bit more familiar with the park before the real work started when the hedgehogs arrived at dusk. In 1839, the grounds of Eglinton hosted the UK's last tournament, an attempt to rekindle knightly sensibilities, complete with jousting and armour. All it did was bankrupt the family. The heavens opened, drenched the crowds and a report from the time was rather damning in the faintness of its praise: 'Two knights ran towards each other, at a very moderate pace indeed, and attempted to poke each other with their poles, mistakenly called lances, in a manner so utterly harmless that a child need scarcely have dreaded the encounter. Not a single knight was unseated, or even made to reel in the saddle.'

The grand house is now derelict and, while the grounds are maintained, the car parks are used for practices that might have caused Lord Archibald Eglinton to 'reel in his saddle' and consider if it was really worth the effort to rekindle chivalry. When I first searched the internet for information about Eglinton, I was presented with the best dogging locations in Ayrshire. Apparently the top car park is better.

Preparing for the first night in the field was exciting. It was so long since I had been out tracking hedgehogs, following their little lives, having the chance to be close to them and get to know them. And now I was doing it from a luxurious base and with the eager help of Douglas.

Actually, having Douglas there did put on a little pressure. It was over ten years since I had done any serious radio-tracking and I did not want to show myself up in front of him.

So when one of the first hedgehogs we released vanished into thin air, I had a feeling that it might all go horribly wrong. In the end the only possible explanation was that her transmitter didn't work properly, unless she had developed the power of flight.

With all twenty hedgehogs out in the park, we fell into a routine. Sleep from 4 a.m. to 10 a.m. (if lucky), breakfast, write up data, lunch, check day nests, supper and back out at 9 p.m. While out radio-tracking the aim was to weigh all the hedgehogs. This would give us a good indication of how they were coping with their new life on the mainland.

 I felt revivified – working outside, close to nature, getting muddy and tired, it was glorious. At least, that is how I was remembering it until I reread some of the diary entries I made: strange how time can moderate memories of hardship.

I had completely forgotten how much I hate Araldite, the glue we used to attach the transmitters to the spines of the hedgehogs. My fingers were raw for days. And the sleep, I had really managed to hide that away in my subconscious, but there is one entry that sums up a lot of how I was feeling in the first week or two: 'Sleeping 0400–0900 is not enough.'

There were other complications. The leads for the receivers were unpredictable, as were the aerials. And it rained a lot. Not only does this make the work harder, wet vegetation hindering the signal, but, as I began to remember from earlier sessions in the rain, the radio receivers come with the strict injunction DO NOT EXPOSE TO MOISTURE.

Inevitably the receivers got damp and inevitably they stopped working. In a particularly poor spell of weather we benefited mightily from Douglas's girlfriend's car. We would find a hog, then get back into the car and stick the receiver on the hot-air blower for twenty minutes.

The hedgehogs: well, they behaved like normal hedgehogs, but they also gave me one hell of a fright. This entire exercise was undertaken in order to see if rescued Uist hedgehogs were unusual: whether they fulfilled the SNH prediction of 'slow and lingering death'. I have to be honest and admit there was a part of me that wondered whether the hedgehog rescuers were going to have to eat a little humble hedgehog pie. SNH had been so determined that there was reason to cull that, even though this contradicted my own work, I was apprehensive.

The first morning after the release we headed out to find the day nests. Most were easy to locate but one signal came from a dense rhododendron bush. Struggling into the depths was hard work, but I needed to check that hedgehog number 234 was in one piece. If only she had been. I pushed under another branch and was suddenly confronted with a headless corpse. I found her snout to one side and her lower jaw a bit further away. I pulled her out and we had a chance to see what had happened. I think it must have been a dog, as a wild predator would have been foolish to leave such a meal. I can imagine a dog rushing into the undergrowth and being called back by their human, unable to finish what they had started.

At least this was not a slow and lingering death.

Two days later, Douglas came back from the day-nest check looking grim. He had found the remains of hog number 274, just the skin and spines with the transmitter still attached. There was no mistaking the grubby pawprint of Mr Brock.

This was confusing. I had been assured that none of the rangers had ever seen a badger in the park. But as the weeks passed, it dawned on me how this contradiction could exist. There is a transition in the park – the rangers leave, there is a pause and then comes trouble. So whether it was the quad-bikers forcing us to dive into the undergrowth, the NEDs ('non-educated delin-quents' – a rather pejorative shorthand used by the locals) with their Buckfast Tonic Wine, the lunatics with torches so bright that they singe the retina and dogs so demented as to make you wish for a gun, the fires that are lit and the rubbish that is left, the rangers just leave well alone and clear up in the morning.

So, the rangers were being quite honest about never seeing a badger in the park because they were never in the park at night.

Then the next night . . . why do I do this? I started to name the hedgehogs, slowly, and the first to be named was Blondie. She was, unsurprisingly, rather blonde. And we found her floating in the small river that runs through the park. Hedgehogs can swim pretty well, but they cannot swim forever, hence the need to provide escape ramps from ponds.

Blondie must have struggled and struggled to get out of the steep-banked brook. The only way I could get her body was to dangle, Douglas holding on to a tree with one hand and the strap of my Barbour bag with the other. Thank you, Barbour, for your reinforced stitching.

After the initial flurry of disappointment, things settled down and I began to relish the night, the noises amplified by the loss of light, especially the sedge warblers, fighting in song over their patches of reed bed.

But I would have liked more moon. Previous hedgehog forays have occurred with a goodly degree of moon. Moon shadows gladden the heart when you are out all night. But this April was poorly provisioned and it left me feeling quite lonely. The moon, when given a chance by the clouds, was shirking, heading for the horizon before the sky had properly darkened.

One night I bumped into an old man who lived alone in a very isolated little cottage in the middle of the park. 'You saving up for a TV?' he said as he saw me approach with the radio-tracking aerial.

Beyond his cottage was a farm, the new home of hedgehog number 385. I had to walk through a field of bullocks and it was like going into an unfamiliar inn and having everything fall silent as the locals just stop and look.

I did not linger after checking the hedgehog was in a proper nest. And she seemed pretty settled, staying around the farm for a few days, keeping her weight up, until one day I found her lying dead in the middle of a field. I bagged her up and cycled back to the cottage with the corpse dangling from my handlebars.

This one really needed an autopsy. The next morning I headed over to Hessilhead and persuaded Andy Christie, one of the founders of the sanctuary, to have a look and see if there was anything obviously wrong. I flexed her limbs and Andy just touched the tight flesh with the new scalpel blade. She opened up easily. 'Oh, they are so like a mole,' Andy exclaimed as he started to root around inside her. Peering over his shoulder, it was easy to see why it is so fascinating. A mole and a hedgehog could not appear more different, but the way they are set up on the inside is remarkably similar.

There was food in her gut, so she had still been eating. There were a few nodules on her lungs that might have interfered with her breathing. Then we saw a marble-sized lump attached to the bladder. It was hard and was obstructing the flow of urine. This poor hedgehog had a tumour. While it was sad to lose another hedgehog, at least it was clear that this beast had died from a pre-existing condition.

Still I was nervous. The project seemed to be haemorrhaging hedgehogs and I was going to have to admit that, perhaps, SNH was right to order a cull. But the rest of the month passed without major mishap. The odd run-in with NEDs on quad bikes added a frisson of danger. But I was getting fitter and relishing being out in the relative wild. A robin flew into the cottage as I was writing up my notes. I caught it and marvelled at how little there is inside the puff of feathers. The data were, despite the losses, looking good. If you discounted events that were unrelated to the fact that the animals had been translocated, such as the pre-existing tumour or the run-in with a badger, then the survival rate was 80 per cent – and if I included all the mortality, then there was still a two-thirds survival – quite good when compared to the 100 per cent death rate of those being captured by SNH.

Nearly all the remaining hedgehogs were steadily increasing in weight. They were regularly seen courting with the resident hogs and they were shifting around the park with increased confidence.

The project had to end and the last night was horrendous. We needed to find each hedgehog and clip off the transmitter so that it could be reused. But it was pouring with rain. The receiver would work briefly before succumbing to the torrents, at which point we would have to retreat to the car to stick it on the blower for a while.

Eventually all were collected and I returned home to begin the task of making sense of what I had found and to get it published in a scientific journal, as without that it lacked credibility.

I was pleased. Pat Morris, who had helped guide that project, was pleased. Most of the losses were due to factors that seemed unrelated to the translocation, there was no evidence of the predicted curl up and die behaviour, most of them put on weight and even the wild hedgehogs we caught seemed to be putting on weight as well. But would it stand up to the scrutiny of our peers. The peer-review process is vital, other academics, referees, getting a chance to peer at scientific papers before they are published.

It took a little time to reach publication, not helped by being messed around by one journal that turned out to have links with a principal proponent of the cull. But eventually *Lutra* took the paper on board and published it in early 2007, precipitating a chain of events that rapidly resulted in a complete transformation in the fate of the Uist hedgehogs.

The rescuers had long recognized that they could not go head to head with SNH; there was too much baggage from the early part of the campaign, especially the decision to describe UHR as animal rights militants. This made it almost impossible for the board of SNH to accede to any demands for fear of creating an apparent precedent of conceding to extremists.

So we did not focus our pressure on SNH. Using a tactic that I am sure is detailed in Sun Tzu's *Art of War*, we looked for the weak link. SNH would not be able to cull without the support of the SSPCA. We knew that, privately, the SSPCA wanted to distance themselves from the cull, despite initial support, but needed new evidence to make the change in policy. And we had that, published in a peer-reviewed scientific journal, so SSPCA withdrew their support, leaving SNH in an impossible position.

The case for the defence was further improved when Stephen Harris published his data, supporting our argument. And then Digger Jackson returned to the fray and argued that the total population of hedgehogs was actually just 3,000, less than half his original prediction – and this following seven years of repro-duction. What on earth was going on here? It really felt as if the entire SNH policy was based on a series of staggeringly erroneous assumptions – resulting in the unnecessary execution of 658 hedgehogs.

Very quickly, the press picked up on the story, and then we got the exciting news we had hoped for; SNH were going to reconsider their position.

This might seem like a complete volte-face, but it is what some of SNH had been yearning for. Meeting a senior scientist at a conference, it became evident that she wanted shot of the cull as much as the rescuers did. She was livid that the situation had taken so long to resolve, and in particular she was upset that unsubstantiated claims had been made by the PR department as to the expected fate of translocated hedgehogs. She had asked them not to claim they would suffer slow and lingering deaths.

But as soon as the claims about this and the allegedly unsavoury nature of the rescuers were made, SNH was in a fix. And it took us to bail them out. Not only had we managed to get the cull stopped, but in 2007 and 2008 SNH actually worked with UHR to relocate live animals from the islands. So begins a new chapter of cooperation.

This still leaves the question of whether the birds will benefit. It feels that everyone has forgotten about the reason for removing the hedgehogs, concentrating instead on the method of removal. Was it even the hedgehogs that were responsible? Why were there similar declines in bird numbers on neighbouring islands that lack hedgehogs? Has global warming had an impact on chick survival by affecting the amount of food available for the parents?

Can hedgehogs and birds ever get along? Obviously they have been at this game for far longer than we have been interfering. But we have altered the environment in such a way as to make any impact of hedgehogs all the more serious. I would argue that even if there are conflicts, as we have seen here, hedgehogs should be given a fair hearing. It may be that they are not the sole causes of any local difficulties or it may be that they do need to be removed. And if that is the case it is vital that we do not just think about welfare, but also about rights.

Hedgehogs arouse passion. It is not always affectionate, but there is something in the manner of the hedgehog that can win people over, even when they are fully aware of the damage that the hogs might cause. Is this a purely British thing? Do we have a nostalgic passion for the animal that harks back to a time when, we imagine, everyone was a bit more like a hedgehog? Busy, industrious, honest and kind; rather like Mrs Tiggy-Winkle. Is our reaction to hedgehogs entirely down to Beatrix Potter?

Of course, the answer is a little more complicated than just being the result of that wonderful woman. There are deep reasons why hedgehogs are such a popular animal.

And is there a way to study hedgehogs and yet avoid a depressing lack of social life? On North Ronaldsay I would find myself confronted with the sound of the seal being broken on a bottle of whisky, accompanied by, 'You'll stay for a small one?' I did try it, but a mist of spirit does not help in the hunt for hedgehogs.

CHAPTER
FOUR

*Hedgehogs
and
People*

Manifestations of hedgehog love are manifold.

I think it is becoming quite clear that it is impossible to have a purely 'natural' history of hedgehogs, at least with me at the helm. Hedgehogs and people are inextricably linked; it is not just me who has been seduced. Hundreds, possibly thousands of people are active hedgehog carers, taking sick and injured animals in and patching them up for release. In fact, if it were not for them, I would not have been required to get quite so up close personal with Nigel and his colleagues – and then what would have become of me?

Take a look around your area and the chances are high that there will be a hedgehog carer nearby. A seemingly marginal activity is actually quite an industry. This is not a new phenomenon. There have always been people who will take pity on a lame or stranded animal, and nurse it back to health before setting it free. But it was always an amateur activity – fairly random and hardly organized. So how has it come to the point that there are 600 carers registered with the British Hedgehog Preservation Society?

St Tiggywinkles Wildlife Hospital in Buckinghamshire claims

to be the first and busiest wildlife hospital in the world. Established in 1985 by Les Stocker, it now treats over 10,000 animals each year, the majority of which, and the clue is in the name, are hedgehogs. Though I do wonder whether they ran the name past the Vatican ... can we beatify at will?

Since then amazing progress has been made; perhaps there is divine oversight after all. Stocker started with a few cardboard boxes and now has an outfit of gleaming steel and uniformed staff bringing in around £1 million each year. But when I went to see him in early January 2008, he was muttering. There were over 500 hedgehogs in residence and he wanted to see the back of them. These were mostly 'autumn orphans' – and as soon as the weather perked up a bit, they would be out in the wild – scattered around the gardens of suburbia. But for now they were just being demanding – of space and time. Racks of cages of hedgehogs, pretty much from floor to ceiling, dominated the convalescence wing.

As he took me round the hospital, he showed me into an operating theatre that was far better equipped than those in many developing countries for people. On the table was an unconscious badger having root canal surgery.

This is top-of-the-range stuff and most places I have visited are not as well catered for. But my unscientific survey of wildlife carers around the country has led me to the conclusion that there are two breeds. There are those like Stocker and his gang who are generalists and take in pretty much any indigenous (and sometimes not so indigenous) beast. And then there are the hedgehog carers, who are, clearly, rather more specific.

And I find that rather fascinating. There are hundreds of people out there who obviously love wildlife, but have dedicated their energies to just one species. Hedgehogs really do attract a different level of attention from any other animal. The very fact that there is a 'Preservation Society' (is it just me, or does this sound a little like somewhere to make jam?) is a case in point. It was set up in 1982 by a retired major, Adrian Coles, who had been bothered by sight of dead hedgehogs in cattle grids, so he launched a campaign to insert ramps and that kick-started the BHPS into life.

There are other animal groups, badger trusts, bat clubs and myriad birding organizations – but they are all rather removed from their subject. I have not found exclusive badger hospitals, otter pharmacies or peregrine physiotherapists.

And if proof were needed of the human–hedgehog relationship, before heading back to help with the badger, Stocker took me to his Hedgehog Museum. Here was clear evidence of a fascination with hedgehogs stretching back thousands of years.

Even before the ancient Egyptians produced scaraboid amulets in hedgehog form, the Mesopotamians were at it. I am sure that hibernation was key to the interest. In civilizations that believed in reincarnation an animal that apparently died each winter only to emerge, reborn, the following spring was going to attract attention. So hedgehog fascination has considerable pedigree.

The museum catalogues just about every conceivable use – and, I have to say, quite a few inconceivable ones – of the hedgehog, or the hedgehog's name, throughout history. From battle formations and tank defences to bottle racks and hairstyles, the hedgehog is everywhere.

Some of the most profound philosophy has sprung from hedgehogs – well, maybe not them personally, but certainly on their behalf. The earliest evidence of this comes from the ancient Greek poet and warrior Archilochus. Fragments of his work have been found and include a wonderful insight into life, mediated via an understanding of hedgehogs:

πόλλ' οἶδ' ἀλώπηξ ἀλλ' ἐχῖνος ἓν μέγα

This has been interpreted, with subtle differences, on many occasions, but the essence is 'The fox knows many things, the hedgehog knows one big thing.' Another version is 'A fox knows many things, but the hedgehog only one: one good one.' I think my favourite is the version that has drifted into an Arabic proverb: 'One knavery of the hedgehog is worth more than many of the fox.'

While the simple interpretation of this is that the prickly ball of a hedgehog flummoxes the wily fox, the idea has taken wings and developed a life, and philosophy, all of its own.

That can be laid at the door of Isaiah Berlin, whose 1953 essay 'The Hedgehog and the Fox' has spawned many other ideas. Berlin argues that while this observation from Archilochus could simply be applied to the behaviour of two species, 'the words can be made to yield a sense in which they mark one of the deepest differences which divide writers and thinkers, and, it may be, human beings in general'.

Our little hedgehog is developed as a metaphor to encompass great thinkers 'who relate everything to a single central vision . . .' I love the way that Berlin is able to run off a list of writers and define them with such a broad sweep of his intellectual brush. 'Plato, Lucretius, Pascal, Hegel, Dostoevsky, Nietzsche, Aristotle, Ibsen, Proust are, in varying degrees hedgehogs . . .' The foxes include the likes of Shakespeare, Goethe and Joyce.

There is a business book called *Good to Great* that has a chapter dedicated to 'The Hedgehog Concept'. The author, Jim Collins, took the Berlin idea and argued that hedgehogs simplify a complex world into a single amazing idea.

> Those who built the good-to-great companies were, to one degree or another, hedgehogs. They used their hedgehog nature to drive forward what we came to call a hedgehog concept for their companies. Those who led the comparison companies tended to be foxes, never gaining the clarifying advantage of a Hedgehog Concept, being instead scattered, diffused and inconsistent.

A psychologist developed a 'hedgehog theory of behaviour'. In one book there is a chapter entitled 'The Concept of Arousal in the Hedgehog', which is almost worth buying the book for alone. Having had a look at it, though, I can imagine some very disappointed hedgehogs in the hedgerow cyber café, searching for online thrills and being confronted with important statements such as, 'The fox has more solutions than they have problems.'

My favourite aphorism is simple, though: clever foxes and wise hedgehogs.

And it is a wise hedgehog who finds a way to get taken in by Caroline Gould at Vale Wildlife Rescue in Gloucestershire. Caroline Gould caters for all sorts. As I walked through the hospital on my way to meet her I passed snakes, turtles, rabbits and little owls. The foxes skulked at the back of their enclosure – adolescents ready for release – but the buzzard was tame, resident and very beautiful.

The wildest animal was, thankfully, locked away. The hospital has been broken into a few times, but not since Fluffy took over security. He is left to roam the corridors at night and is one of the obstacles that any new member of staff has to overcome. If you can work with Fluffy even the fiercest arrivals will be a pushover.

Not sure if his name really is Fluffy, we were not introduced. The guard dog just glared at me through the door's window, thankfully reinforced, in between fits of frenzied, fang-flashing rage.

Like most wildlife carers, Caroline started as an amateur, operating out of the back garden of her semi-detached home. Back in the early 1980s there were sanctuaries for cats and dogs, even farm animals, but nothing for wildlife. Individuals took in the waifs and strays of the hedgerow, nursing them back to health before sending them on their way, but it was haphazard; no one had this as a job. And that is important. Caroline soon found that if you let the local police and RSPCA know you take in wild animals, the word gets out. And then the local press will pick up on the story, because it is easy to get good copy from wildlife carers. So more people come to you with the animals they find, and what do you do? Turn away patients because you have to go out to earn a living? Or start at least trying to cover your costs by getting donations? Before long you become a charity, and while your head has been down as you remove fly eggs from a damaged hedgehog, the world shifts and, when you look up, you find this has become your life.

With absolute determination Caroline has built a mini-empire, from kitchen-sink operations to an operating theatre. From one tawny owl to 5,000 animals a year in a purpose-built hospital near Tewkesbury, Gloucestershire.

'When I started this I would have laughed at the idea I would be managing ten staff and running a hospital in twenty-three years' time.' She has also managed to raise a family, somehow. 'Three kids, animals are much easier, they have all flown the nest, and so has my husband. He gave me an ultimatum, either the animals go or he goes. Took me a good thirty seconds to think that one through. So here I am, and I don't regret it in the slightest.'

What got Caroline fired up was hearing so often that people would leave an injured animal 'to let nature take its course'. Still she flares at the thought. 'How could it be left to nature when most of the problems are caused by people?' So that is what drove her to make this massive commitment, raising money, cajoling local businesses and spreading the word.

One of the most important tasks, though, is to develop a

good and trusting relationship with a vet. Many carers struggle because of the difficulty of finding a vet who is suitably enthusiastic. Certainly this is something that Caroline found. 'When we began, attitudes were totally different and we were just regarded as animal "nutters" wasting our time on wildlife.' But attitudes have changed and now she has an excellent relationship with one vet in particular who steps in to do those things she and her staff cannot manage.

But it is a two-way relationship. Now vets from around the country contact Caroline to get advice on how to treat the wild animals they have encountered. The expertise at Vale is such that much of the work is done by the staff now – and thanks to the fund-raising, most equipment is on-site, saving animals a stressful journey to the vet, just leaving the vet with a stressful journey to them, and Fluffy.

The centre is constantly busy. Like a human hospital, staff have to be on hand twenty-four hours a day, every day. Casualties can, and do, appear at any time; cleaning, feeding and medicating the patients form a constant round. During early summer baby hedgehogs from disturbed nests can threaten to flood the system, as they require feeding every two hours.

The amount of food they get through is staggering, well over 1,000 tins of pet food a week, mealworms by the bucket, (dead) day-old chicks by the sack, maggots, fruit, fish, insects and the

 rest of it – and that is before you consider the drugs that are needed.

Why does she do it? It is not as if she ever gets any gratitude from the wildlife. 'But when you

release an animal you know you are doing the right thing, even though it is just a drop in the ocean.'

Caroline is not sentimental about her charges and has learned the hard way that it is often better to euthanize earlier than later. There are animals that she would once have kept alive that she will now kill on arrival: 'I know other centres disagree, but I believe that wildlife has no quality of life in captivity. I will work on an animal for days, weeks or months if I think it can go back into the wild.'

Even her very first charge, the one-winged tawny owl, would not have escaped this more severe attitude. It would have been put down straight away.

The same goes for hedgehogs. Many centres will release three-legged hogs back into the wild, as long as it is a rear leg that's missing (without the front leg they cannot feed, so they cannot be released). But as recently as last year Caroline has changed the policy at Vale: 'We began to notice that three-legged hedgehogs were coming in with parasites congregating on the side with the missing leg, mainly ticks that they were not able to remove by scratching. So now we euthanize them as well.'

Hedgehogs are the most common mammal, but Caroline is worried that she has been seeing fewer brought in. This is evidence of a real decline, as there are more people interested in the hospital bringing in other species, so it's just that they are finding fewer hedgehogs. She used to get over 1,000 hedgehogs each year; now it is 700 and the trend continues downwards.

It is not only the number of hedgehogs that

is causing her concern, but also their health. 'I call them "clangers",' she explained. 'They first appeared in 1999. They are hyperactive. They have a different shape, a narrower head. You can tell they are clangers as soon as you see them.' None of them live to maturity and, despite numerous autopsies, no cause has been found. Alarmingly, she is now seeing up to forty a year.

In fact, Caroline is concerned that the health of wildlife in general is deteriorating. Many birds are arriving in poor shape. 'I think there is a toxic time bomb out there, just the build-up of all sorts of poisons we are pouring into the environment.'

Though what caused her most remarkable hedgehog, Bandit, to be quite as he was remains a complete mystery. He had a 5-centimetre stripe across his back that was so black and glossy they at first assumed it was paint. But no amount of scrubbing would remove this blemish and the spines grew true – normal colour everywhere else, but rich black on the band.

They kept him in captivity, reasoning that they would be able to look after him better than anyone else, and he was so unusual that he would inevitably attract attention. Untoward interest in her hogs was something that Caroline has had to contend with before. 'About ten years ago I was approached by someone offering to buy every hedgehog I could lay my hands on for pets. They offered me £200 per hedgehog.' I had heard rumours, but not met anyone who had actually been on the receiving end of an approach. I asked if she had taken it any further, but she had just dismissed it out of hand.

She is not alone in being approached. An exotic pet dealer from

Calgary, Canada, went to a great deal of trouble in his attempt to secure breeding stock, even managing to obtain an import permit.

Caroline has had no further attempts to obtain our hedgehogs for the pet trade, but there has been a boom over the Atlantic in keeping pygmy hedgehogs. Has Caroline seen any evidence of that in the UK? 'I've never met a pygmy hedgehog, but I have seen adverts for them for sale and often get people calling me up to see if I have any I can spare as pets. They get short shrift. I do not believe that hedgehogs should be kept as pets.'

But attitudes do change. And while it might seem odd, repugnant even, to keep hedgehogs as pets, it would not be the first time that there has been such a dramatic change in our relationship with them. I believe there is a point in history about which all this turns. The year 1905 is perhaps the most significant in hedgehog history. That was when hedgehogs went from portent to paragon.

Prior to that momentous date attitudes towards hedgehogs were dictated by their love of the dark and their secretive behaviour. They were very much creatures of the wild.

As far back as the Bible, hedgehogs are associated with the wilderness that haunts the remnants of Nineveh – the city destroyed by God in judgement for their pride (or by the Babylonians as they helped end the Assyrian empire). Though there is a slight problem with this – which calls into question much of the content of the Bible. Hedgehogs only appear in some translations. In others the word is given as porcupine or, worse still, bittern. Now, at a push I can see the confusion between a spiny rodent and a spiny insectivore – but a heron? Given this dramatic confusion, what else might be amiss?

Early hedgehog references from the UK echo some of the other fairy tales that were perpetuated as fact. Pliny the Elder, repeating and embellishing Aristotle, claimed that hedgehogs were blessed with great weather-predicting capabilities. Very easy really – as long as you find a hedgehog that has made an underground home with more than one entrance. Then just watch to see which hole gets blocked and you can learn where the weather is coming from. This has been extrapolated into Groundhog Day – possibly – as some persist in the fiction that 2 February is actually the ancient festival of Hedgehog Day.

And then there are the fruit-collecting habits. *The Aberdeen Bestiary* from around AD 1200 recreates this with a detailed image that, when you give it any thought, is obviously absurd. How could hedgehogs collect fruit on their spines?

I suppose you can imagine someone seeing hedgehogs snuffling around rotting apples in the autumn, as this will be where a host of slugs and insects collect, so perhaps this could be confused with an attempt to eat the fruit, and hedgehogs will eat a little fruit. And there must have been considerable mystery surrounding an animal that did not emerge to eat for many months. Surely it must have a stock of food stored away to tide it through the rigours of winter? Well, it does, as we all know, though not in the form of a well-stocked pantry, but with a subcutaneous larder – layers of fat under the skin.

If, just if, a hedgehog was to go about gathering fruit, how would it do that? Well, it does collect vegetation, dragging it into the day nest or hibernaculum, not on its spines but with its mouth. And you need to think a bit about a hedgehog collecting fruit on its spines – there are problems. How easy would it be for a hedgehog to roll up and then propel itself into some fruit? Not very. The rationalist might argue that this was a chance encounter between falling fruit and a slug-eating hog, oblivious at the foot of a tree. But again – no. For the fruit to become impaled there must be some erect spines. But a happy hedgehog, halfway through a slug, is not going to have a care in the world, while the silent approach of the apple is hardly going to generate an erection of prickles. And a hedgehog would have difficulty walking in such a state.

Where was I? Early imaginings of hedgehogs.

It is inevitable that an animal as secretive and night-loving as the hedgehog is going to attract the attention of the myth-creator. While they have not become the bogey-beast of nightmares, they have proved their power as portent.

The bad luck that emanates from a nocturnal hedgehog encounter was recounted in the *Folk-Lore Journal* in 1889. A Mr Macpherson, from near the River Spey, passed this local superstition to the journal:

> I was returning home about midnight, and, when on the bridge crossing the Tulchan Burn at Straan, met a hedgehog. Next day, I, in jest, asked some of the older people if there was any superstition connected with such a meeting. They told me it

was unlucky, and seemed to predict some calamity to myself. Two nights after a girl was drowned in the Spey, not far from the scene of my meeting with the hedgehog.

The entry goes on to reveal that the hedgehog and the drowning of the girl were connected, and no amount of arguing could drive the idea from the minds of the people who believed the girl went in the place of the person that met the animal.

Hedgehogs were also considered wise. The 1872 publication *Zoological Mythology* describes how:

> The Arabs are accustomed to say that the champion of truth must have the courage of the cock, the scrutiny of the hen, the heart of the lion, the rush of the wild boar, the cunning of the fox, the prudence of the hedgehog, the swiftness of the wolf, the resignation of the dog, and the complexion of the naguir.

Do snakes have good complexions? I wonder what they use? And not just wisdom. They ooze health-giving properties, sometimes literally, with the Gypsy traditions of using smoke from burning the spines of a hedgehog as a cold cure, and Hungarian Gypsies also used the ash from burnt spines to help heal wounds. Hedgehog fat and sometimes urine were smeared on as a cure for rheumatism.

And as for toothache, a farmer was reported in 1915 as having complete faith in the power of the hedgehog. When troubled, he took the jawbone of a hedgehog, wrapped in fine cloth, and kept it in his waistcoat pocket, on the side of the painful tooth, and would never be parted from it, as the pain never returned following the intervention of the hedgehog.

Perhaps more worryingly, in these relatively enlightened times, is the story from a website that may or may not be reputable – but that is beside the point, as the contents are worth repeating even if a complete hoax. Apparently a thirty-five-year-old Serbian man needed emergency surgery after he tried to have sex with a hedgehog on the advice of a witchdoctor who claimed it would cure premature ejaculation. The animal was unhurt and the hospital managed to repair the man's damaged organ.

OK, stop thinking about the last example for a minute and let me tell you that I have found a way in which hedgehogs do help cure people. As I have gradually met more people who care for hedgehogs I have grown to believe that there are some who are gaining as much from the hedgehogs as the hedgehogs are gaining from them, if not more.

Janis Dean's hedgehog hospital is hidden away in the very neat suburbs of Poulton-le-Fylde, Lancashire. She likes it that way and is not keen on too much attention. It is as far removed from St Tigs or Vale as you could imagine. This is her home, not some hospital. And she is only interested in hedgehogs. And her dog is much more friendly.

Janis's front room is stuffed with hedgehogabilia. Every possible hedgehogable item is hedgehogged. It made me realize that I was missing out on so much – tea towels, keyrings, paperweights, cards, warning signs, earrings and much (too) much more. For two weeks of the year she has use of a charity shop in Blackpool, but that means much of the rest of the year her home becomes a warehouse. One day, she hopes, all this stuff will find its way into a new shed and she will begin to reclaim at least part of her life.

That is not going to happen any time soon, as she is always in demand, usually for European hedgehogs. But a few days before I arrived in September 2007, Janis had a visit from one of the singers down on Blackpool Pier. The singer had been given a gift by an adoring fan, one that she did not know how to deal with. The gift, a pet hedgehog, sat in a cage on the bar in her club for a couple of weeks while she pondered what to do, before finding out about Janis.

'He is ever so grumpy,' Janis warned me as we went through the house to the converted shed. Her hedgehog hospital was so ordered, clean and clutter-free. 'This is such a relief, having a separate place for the hogs,' she said. Until she had it built everything was done at the kitchen sink, cleaning out wounds, picking off maggots. The hospital was built thanks to the generosity of businesses in the area. She had written to everyone she could think of. MFI donated worktops, a local tiling company did the floor and a roofing company the roof. 'There was only one local company that did not want to help, but he went bust soon after.'

The rows of cages in this self-contained unit were purpose-made. She had done a rare piece on the local radio station and got a call from some solicitors who had heard it and were executors of a will. They just asked her what she wanted. And what she wanted was cages.

'I think I went a bit over the top,' she said. 'You could keep a rhino in those, they are so strong.'

She was right about the hedgehog; what a grump – small, blond and filled with indignation for the entire human race. A couple of weeks on the bar in a nightclub must not have helped the mood of this African pygmy hedgehog and he required gloves to be handled, even by Janis.

It was hard to imagine that this species has caused such a stir in America, where they are the pet of choice. I have seen the websites that praise their petability to the heights, but I just can't see it. This little beast was not going to make anyone a good pet. Smaller, very definitcly not 'one of ours', as it had longer ears and was so blond that, if it were not for the dark eyes, it could easily be mistaken for an albino.

Janis seems an unlikely hedgehog carer. 'I really don't know how it started. I had no interest in wildlife, didn't really like animals,' she explained. But there was a sequence of events that gave things an inevitability.

It began in 1990. Overworked at the civil service, faced with a job move and promotion while living with her son at her mother's and working in a petrol station at night to try to get enough money together to buy a house, 'everything went "boom" and I've never been the same again. The doctor told me to go home and watch the grass grow. I did.'

And as she watched the grass, she began to

notice droppings, hedgehog droppings. These are distinctive: frequently quite shiny as a result of the exoskeletons of the insects they munch up passing through their gut, they usually have one end quite blunt and the other more pointed. Not much more than a couple of centimetres long, they will often be the first indication you get of a spiky resident.

There can be a bizarre fascination with hedgehog poo. I was at a friend's party recently when I noticed some on the patio. I went in to tell them and they wanted to see, so I led them out and explained why this was hedgehog poo. Word spread and I then spent the next half an hour accompanying at least ten other people and giving a series of impromptu lectures on the digestive system of the hedgehog.

Janis extended her grass-watching to the night in an attempt to see the defecators, and this is when she noticed that the hedgehogs were coming into her garden through a hole in her neighbour's fence. A short time later he started to replace the old fence and refused to leave a gap for Janis's nightly visitors. This sparked an interest that was to draw her out of her depression, and when she found a baby hedgehog late one autumn, her path to recovery was set out before her.

She did everything you are supposed to, kept it warm and well fed, bought a heat pad and transformed a rabbit hutch into a hedgehog home. By spring the hedgehog was fat and healthy and ready for release. Very quickly the word got out that there was a hedgehog lady on the block and she has not had a moment's peace since.

For Janis the relationship is reciprocal. 'Initially the hedgehogs helped me. I couldn't go out and didn't want to see anyone, and they have helped me get over that,' she said quietly. 'If I didn't have this I don't know what I would do. I can't hold a job down. I don't like . . . I just don't like people. I haven't had good experiences with people.'

There is a deep sadness within Janis; she is a remarkable woman, working so hard. 'Everything I'd done previously I'd dabble at and then get fed up. But this is it. This is what I want to do.'

I asked her about the appeal of hedgehogs. She paused and then said, 'Well, it's the whole package: how they look, how they behave, how they tolerate so much pain, how they let you care for them. I am sure they know I am trying to help. They just don't do any harm. They just get on with doing good, out of sight.' Rather like Janis, I feel.

There are those who might consider Janis extreme. She is not. On a scale of hedgehog carers, she would barely register when seen next to Barbara Roberts.

Her 1930s end-of-terrace house in the Manchester suburb of Withington, south of the centre, gives nothing away. In fact I cycled right past the first time.

Retracing my steps, I noticed a discreet sign identifying the home of Withington Hedgehog Care and a large cuddly hog, but there was still no real indication of what to expect. I was a bit disappointed, for I was expecting something rather more dramatic. The stories I had heard left me imagining that the property would be mired in the smell of hedgehogs. I had imagined that it would be down a forgotten lane and that there would be a pack of feral dogs patrolling the perimeter. I pictured mud and chaos and mess.

I followed the noise of busy-ness. And there was Barbara, opening tins of dog food, chatting to the hedgehogs in the rows of cages stacked behind her in one of three small garden sheds. She was slow on her feet – there was a walking stick nearby – but she was constantly moving, cleaning out food bowls, filling food bowls and talking to her charges. The shed had pet carriers stacked from floor to ceiling. This was not a busy time, she told me. 'You should have been here earlier in the year. I've only got about 200 hedgehogs here now.' Over winter she had peaked at 463 hedgehogs in these three sheds and throughout her very ordinary home. I started counting the cages – yes, there were enough to accommodate this number. For once it looked like the reports of hedgehog numbers were about right.

She stopped and offered to make some tea. I winced quietly, as she seemed to have little concern for her own well-being. Maybe she did wash her hands in between cleaning the bowls of old food and new faeces, but I didn't see her do it. Luckily some of the biscuits she offered were individually wrapped.

Barbara's life has been besieged by sadness and ill health, but she has found solace in hedgehogs, and thousands of hedgehogs have found solace in her. She has a nurturing zeal that has taken her through a demanding career in nursing while also caring for her parents at home. But it is her earlier experience with abuse and breakdown that seems to lie at the heart of this transference of care from humans to animals.

The more we talk about why she is so fascinated with hedgehogs, the closer to tears she gets. There is something very painful in her life that might have destroyed a less resilient person, or at least forced them to turn in on themselves.

'I just can't bear to see an animal in pain,' she said as we returned to the task of cleaning and feeding. 'So the first thing I do with any sick hedgehog is to make it as comfortable as possible.'

Barbara has an impressive arsenal of drugs and equipment. There is a cabinet of stainless-steel implements and packets of disposable syringes; in fact, the room looks like a mini operating theatre.

Over the years hedgehog carers have developed techniques for dealing with sickness and injury. Medicines for other animals have been tried on hedgehogs and treatments that work spread around the informal network. While there might be some disputes about style between carers, they do seem to be willing to share ideas of what will and will not work. For example, the painkiller Metacam is supposed to be used on dogs. With hedgehogs it is just a matter of giving a dose proportional to the weight of the patient.

Is there any testing done? 'Well, I try everything before I give it to the hedgehogs,' Barbara says in a matter-of-fact tone. I express a little surprise, but she continues as if there could be nothing more normal. 'Well, Metacam tastes really quite nice, but they hate one of the antibiotics and I can see why. You know the rehydration mix for animals is frightfully expensive, so I just use human ones. The hedgehogs cannot get enough of the lemon and lime, but hate the blackcurrant.'

Working closely with local vets, carers become adept at diagnoses, and most also become skilled at realizing when they are out of their depth. 'If there is a need for something like an amputation, I will always go straight to my vet,' she explained. 'But I can do so much here.' Though I do not know how much the vets approve of her unorthodox approach to drug testing.

By now the noise in the shed is remarkable as thirty hedgehogs start eating dog food simultaneously. Then her rather deranged dog kicks off again – this dog was in a cage in her bedroom, for my benefit, as it is a little temperamental around people. A van had pulled up from the local pet shop. I helped carry the stacks of tins into a shed. This is where the money goes. Barbara spends pretty much her entire pension on food for the animals. Now she is a registered charity she does get some money coming in, especially when she needs new equipment, but before she got that status she relied on more unorthodox methods of fund-raising.

I had noticed a photograph of John Thaw, an actor famous for his grumpy Inspector Morse. Expecting it to be indicative of a slight crush, I asked what he was doing on the wall. 'Oh, he was one of my regular donors,' Barbara said. 'I wrote to him when I was having difficulties. I just said, "You have a kind face, could you help?" and I got a letter from him and a cheque. I never met him, but I was thrilled to be invited to his memorial service.'

There was also a letter from Buckingham Palace. Barbara wrote to the Queen when she heard about the plans to cull the hedgehogs on the Uists. 'I said, "You are the Queen, you can stop this sort of thing," but I didn't get a reply.' Undaunted Barbara phoned the Palace to complain. 'Well, I didn't get through to Her Majesty, but I spoke to someone who explained that she is very busy. And I did eventually get a letter.'

Barbara takes in hedgehogs from all over Manchester and sometimes further out into Lancashire. And as she does not drive, she is forced to do all this on public transport.

One afternoon, Barbara had a call from an elderly lady about a sick hedgehog she had found out on her lawn. Barbara told her to take it in and keep it warm, put it in a box with a strong light over it alongside a plastic bottle filled with warm water. Shortly before setting off on the two-hour journey to collect the patient, Barbara phoned just to check it was still alive. Yes, said the old lady, I can see it moving.

On arrival Barbara could not help but notice a strong smell. She looked into the box and was shocked to find a very dead hog. But the lady was so pleased with what she had done, picking up the hog in her husband's jumper, that Barbara did not have the heart to tell her that the movement was not the hedgehog but a pulsating mass of maggots that had all started getting more active as the temperature increased.

So Barbara picked up the box and said she had to rush back to get it fixed up. There are certain ways to guarantee getting a double seat on public transport. This was one of them.

It is undeniably the case that Barbara is an eccentric person.

A wonderfully warm, eccentric person who cares passionately about hedgehogs, and not just hedgehogs. She is quite matter of fact as she tells me how she slept with a blind squirrel every night for three years: 'Well, he was just so miserable on his own.'

The more time I spent with Barbara the more it became clear that this is not a one-way process. While she is working tirelessly to aid hedgehogs, in their own quiet way the hedgehogs are keeping Barbara alive. Without drama she commented, 'If it weren't for the hedgehogs, there would be nothing to get out of bed for in the morning.' And that was about more than just dealing with lethargy. I really felt that Barbara would not have recovered from cancer, and would not be able to deal with the catalogue of conditions she currently suffers from, without the hedgehogs. This genuinely is a symbiotic relationship. In fact, I would argue that Barbara and perhaps many others have been self-medicating with hedgehogs for years. And they obviously work . . . Perhaps we could get them on the NHS?

We are back at that idea of the relationship between hedgehogs and people being more complicated than it is between us and most other species. We embrace them in literature; we take them to our bosom (not too tightly) and care for them. And they are everywhere. A hedgehog is one of the most recognized of computer-game characters – Sonic. How did they think of that?

The Japanese development team was seeking an original character for a computer game unlike any other. Their first priority was 'speed' – they wanted a character that would be exhilarating. So they came up with a rabbit (do you think that Sonic the Rabbit would have worked?), but were then stuck with how a rabbit could attack in an exciting way – they wanted to be able to send the character on a 'charge' that would beat an enemy. And what creature could disable the opposition with a fast charge? Why, one covered in spikes. And obviously a porcupine would have just been silly.

Take a step back and have a look for hedgehogs in everyday life. I think you will be surprised at how many there are and where they get to. Beijing zoo's gift kiosk features two species of cuddly toy – the panda, obviously, and the hedgehog. Why? There are just two in the zoo, hidden away in a darkened corridor, sharing space with a cantankerous flying squirrel.

When did hedgehogs suddenly become the symbol for banking? Two banks have been running hedgehog-related campaigns as I write this book.

Icelandic bank Icesave featured a curled-up hedgehog in its adverts – implying what? That, come the winter, the bank will go to sleep for five months and burn up all the fat you have laid down for it? And why has an Icelandic bank taken the hedgehog to heart? There are no hedgehogs in Iceland.

Fortunately Icesave's Alan Gilmour was able to help. 'We liked the image of the hedgehog,' he explained, 'because it communicated so well that with our interest-rate guarantee not only were you well protected as with a hedgehog and its quills, but that you could afford to put your interest in your savings money into hibernation knowing that you would still be protected from cuts in interest rates and that your money would still be getting a great return. The imagery also allowed us to do this in a non-clichéd and unbank-like way. In this instance the hedgehog is meant to represent the customer and not the bank.'

Still not quite sure that works for me.

But the real delight has been Abbey. How did they get the hedgehogs to dance so wonderfully on TV? Shame they would not share that with me – they were worried that I might be concerned about the use of animals in advertising. At least my local branch allowed me to take away a couple of the large cardboard hedgehogs that had featured in their window.

There was some, if rather tenuous, logic connecting banks and hogs. But why did the North Face produce a pair of rugged trainers and call them the Hedgehog? I have tried to get them to explain the reasoning, but have not had an answer (or, more importantly, a pair of the shoes – I thought it might be rather cool to go off radio-tracking hedgehogs in Hedgehogs, though to be honest wellies are far more practical). It makes no sense. These are shoes designed for life at breakneck speed, careering down the side of a mountain, charging up another mountain, yet they carry the moniker of a woodland-loving animal that has a top speed of around 4 km/h and prefers to curl up when confronted by anything too challenging – like a mountain, I imagine.

A more appropriate use was for children's shoes, as I saw in Germany. The upset here was that the range did not extend to adult sizes.

Hedgehogs crop up in all sorts of places. There are the

traditional pipe-cleaning tools called hedgehogs – a sort of reamer that scrapes bits of carbon off the bowl. Black & Decker produced a Hedge Hog, a hedge trimmer.

There was a forge that crafted all sorts of amazing blades. I have a billhook, a kind of English machete that I use for splitting kindling, which was born from the 'Hedgehog Forge'. I noticed it on a market stall – great how your eyes can pick up things at the merest glance – an image of a hedgehog, pressed into the blade. Like scanning text, I can usually find the word hedgehog. The forge was based up in Cannock, Staffordshire, the property of Cornelius Whitehouse, and has produced no end of wonderful blades, particularly, and rather delightfully, for hedge-laying, the now fading art of keeping our landscape truly alive, and keeping hedgehogs happy.

Ironwork is still the domain of some hedgehog-related companies. I was delighted, and a little shocked, to find the Erotic Hedgehog, a company that specializes in the 'bespoke design of wrought iron', complete with restraints. I asked Brian Sims, founder and blacksmith of the Erotic Hedgehog, where he got the idea to rope a hedgehog into the promotion of high-end bondage-tinged internal fittings. 'Well, the Erotic Hedgehog is a very new venture,' he explained. 'We did our first Erotica show this year at Earls Court. But we have been blacksmithing for much longer under the hedgehog banner.'

The Happy Hedgehog Wrought Iron Work is the home of the Erotic Hedgehog. And the Happy Hedgehog goes way back to pre-blacksmith days. 'I had been planning on writing a children's story about a hedgehog family living at the bottom of the garden,' Brian said. 'But then events took over. I was made redundant, became apprenticed to a blacksmith and then took on the company. It was my kids' idea to rename it after the central character in my stories – the Happy Hedgehog.'

And what wise kids. He has had work commissioned simply on the strength of the name alone and even had a call from a professor of business studies to say that it was possibly the best name for a business he had ever come across.

But it was not just his children. 'I suppose it goes back to my childhood,' Brian said. 'I remember that we rescued a little one and looked after it in our garden. I used to rush home from school at the end of the day to check it was OK.' So hedgehogs have become wedged into his psyche and, like so many other people, he has difficulty on putting his finger on the attraction: smelly, flea-ridden, solitary, prickly and nocturnal, they are hardly the recipe for unrestrained, or even restrained, love.

Relying on your children for a company name is not something unique to Brian Sims. The Heavenly Hedgehog Ice Cream Company, from Bethlehem, Pennsylvania, is quite honest about the origins of the name. In fact, their website has a list of answers to frequently asked questions. So the answer to the very first question is, 'It's what happens when you let your children name your store.' I am not sure what the question to answer number six is, though: 'No, there isn't a bed in the back of the store.' Perhaps they just have some very tired customers.

The award for the most inappropriate use of a hedgehog

in advertising, however, must go to Ford – advertising a car through a cute little hedgehog wanting a ride is just so very wrong on so very many levels.

The Department of Transport picked up on a more positive use of the hedgehog. The Green Cross Code is no longer mediated by Darth Vader – the actor who played the part of the Green Cross Code Man, dressed in a superhero outfit, was best known for his portrayal of Luke Skywalker's father (and if you have not seen *Star Wars* movies, sorry for giving away the denouement). No, in 1997 they moved to the far more charismatic hedgehog.

Quite a good arrangement, this. Hedgehogs teach our children to look right, left and then right again, and in return there is a wonderful network of carers to take in and patch up those hedgehogs that fail to heed their own advice.

I have visited carers from the south of England to Scotland and have met some of the most incredible characters along the way. What I am not sure is whether the act of caring for animals in general, and hedgehogs in particular, generates the sorts of person I have met, or whether the sorts of people I have met are the only ones who would become involved.

Take Elaine Drewrey, for example. I had heard her referred to in hushed tones. Just outside the Lincolnshire town of Louth is a village called Authorpe and in the old post office you will find Hedgehog Care, to which she is committed with every last ounce of her being.

When I visited I was greeted by an eyeless dog, with two indentations in his head, nicely covered in fur, where eyes once were. Elaine got him from a place she referred to as the 'death-row dogs', a charity that tries to rehome dogs that would otherwise have been put down.

He is an amazing hound. He uses his nose a great deal – especially as he is pretty deaf as well – but to get about, he picks up one of his plastic toys and holds it in his mouth, out in front of him, like a white stick, knocking it on the ground and everything around him to navigate Elaine's cluttered home.

Elaine has the grubbiest house I have ever been into, but she is not ashamed. There is a notice on the wall: 'I'm not at all offended if humans walk out, but if you feel like you want to help, there are plenty of cloths and dusters.' Few people take up the offer.

And when would she tidy up? The night before I arrived she had been up until 4 a.m. nursing two sick baby hogs – both unfortunately died. In everything, the hedgehogs get priority: they eat before she does, get cleaned before she does.

I asked about the silver disc on the wall – one of those things that adorn the walls of a rock star's home. 'Oh, that's my daughter's band,' she said nonchalantly. This disc commemorated the band, Swing Out Sister, selling 250,000 copies of the song 'Breakout'. Lead singer Corinne Drewery is Elaine's daughter. I remember her as being unattainably glamorous and quite unlikely to be mucking in with her mother. But I was wrong there; Corinne will come when needed. Though she is prone to telling her mother a few home truths, threatening to send her away so she can clear the place up. 'She says stuff like, "People just don't live like this. Why don't you get someone else to come and do the hedgehogs?" But when she comes, well, she doesn't much agree with the disinfectant I use and insists we use white vinegar and herby stuff.'

Elaine continued, 'I know I live in a tip, but my home is also the intensive care unit of the hospital. All the new animals come in here to be assessed. Any that need to, go straight to the vet, even though I know as much about hedgehogs. But I am not allowed to get all the drugs, as I am just a quack housewife. In fact, they often ask my advice. Anyway, no hedgehog has ever complained about the state of the house and that is what matters to me.'

I have to confess that I have never seen a kitchen like hers. There are four boxes on the floor containing sick hogs, there are syringes, medicines and pet food all around and in the sink, while on a shelf there are containers of drugs. I mention that the use-by date on one of the packets is 1999. 'Still works,' Elaine retorts. 'If it works with the hedgehogs I use it. Some of these are banned now. I only give up when the labels drop off and I am not sure what is inside.'

Elaine had about 300 patients last year, but she is getting very bothered, because the number she sees has been steadily dropping. 'Well, it could be that other people have set up their own hospitals, so they are getting the ones I used to. It could be that people just aren't bothering to bring them in, or it could be that there are less hedgehogs out there. I know which I think it is.'

As she explained, 'Most of my hogs came from around Louth, but where there used to be orchards, where there used to be pony paddocks and long gardens, there are just concrete and tarmac now. Hedgehogs can't live without a home and if you crush them into a small space that they have to share with badgers, well, badgers just eat them like cherries. Hedgehogs need their own space.'

So did Elaine's husband. After a move to the country and discovering that when rescued lambs pee on newly laid parquet flooring it explodes, he ran off with a more houseproud, younger model.

'I don't blame him at all,' Elaine adds. 'I had always been picking up animals, but the first hedgehog was Wilfred Pickles, a baby that got left behind when his mum moved her nest after I had disturbed them.'

That was thirty years ago.

'They say with wildlife you shouldn't love it, that you should respect it. But the day I do that is the day I give up,' Elaine said.

While I was there a small gaggle of three girls plus their aunt turned up. None had ever been here before, but this is a regular occurrence for Elaine. Despite the murmurings, she is a favourite with children and she is more than happy to introduce her visitors to the hogs. Watching the little ones' faces light up, it was clear to see why Elaine is a popular attraction. She has a no-nonsense approach, telling the children, without being patronizing, what is going on with the animals she pulls out of their bedding.

As they leave, I hear the tinkle of coins in the collecting box and I ask Elaine how she survives. She leads me round the corner to another building. There is a 'Hogsfam' notice in the window and inside is a charity shop; clothes, books, toys fill the room. Next door is another shed filled with new hedgehog-related merchandise: tea towels, mugs, T-shirts, etc. Every year she has a big sale that brings in some money and then she has some other, surprising patrons.

'The bikers, aren't they wonderful?' she sighed. 'Every April a local motorcycle club comes and does a slow procession, raising money for Hedgehog Care. Such good-hearted leather boys. I've every admiration for them.'

Not all her hedgehogs survive, though, and since she set up the centre in 1985, many hundreds have died. These are buried in a plot that Elaine has set aside for the purpose. There is a stained-glass window set in a brick arch that presides over this graveyard, and a slate with the following prayer carved into it:

> *Goodnight Hedgehog,*
> *Loved briefly by few in our weary world*
> *Of mistakes and indifference.*
> *Wake up with hope in your happy heaven*
> *Of grubs and peace and country treasures,*
> *Where roads and poisons and humans*
> *Will never hurt you or your habitat again. Amen*

And then there is Elaine herself. While she is clear about her future, it is the hedgehogs that cause her worry. 'Well, if I last another ten years before I snuff it, at the rate things are going there won't be any hedgehogs left. So I can curl up my toes knowing there is no more work to do, and all people will be able to do is look at picture of hedgehogs in books.'

That would be a disaster. Elaine is better placed than most to see the impact on people of meeting a hedgehog face to face. 'Children who have held one, that will stay with them for the rest of their lives. I hope that they leave here with a feeling of responsibility for hedgehogs and all wildlife.'

And the reason why they are so good at making this impact goes beyond aesthetics. Yes, Elaine waxes lyrical about their amazing fluffy tummies and cute faces, but she believes there is more. 'You've only got to meet one,' she says. 'Anyone who runs one over and thinks that it is just a hedgehog, they should be made to hold one and look at it nose to nose and realize what they are capable of, how hardy and courageous they are. These are miracle animals.'

So how has this happened? How have hedgehogs gone from creatures of portent to this most loved of animals?

One measure of our attitudes to a species can be seen in literature. And this is where 1905 becomes so significant. Before 1905, hedgehogs appeared – how could they not – in stories aimed at children. Fairy tales cast the hedgehog in a mysterious or mischievous light – the Brothers Grimm used them well, though with some rather adult overtones, Kipling inaccurately imported them to South America for a *Just So* story, but that was all before 1905 and the publication of perhaps the most important book any species has ever starred in, *The Tale of Mrs Tiggy-Winkle.* We are talking year zero spanning two eras

– BBP and ABP: Before Beatrix Potter and After Beatrix Potter. Rarely do I meet someone who does not refer to Mrs Tiggy-Winkle at some point in a discussion about the attraction of hedgehogs.

In fact Ms Potter was even more remarkable than most people realize. Changing our perceptions of wildlife and seriously upping the ante on anthropomorphism were a sideshow for her true, and largely unrequited, love. Beatrix Potter was a scientist, a gifted and intuitive scientist who, if she had been born in less discriminatory times, might have achieved things greater than Mrs Tiggy-Winkle. Tom Wakeford, author of the wonderful book *Liaisons of Life*, describes her story as 'a legend of youthful scientific inquiry stifled by pomposity and prejudice, and of a heresy that was later vindicated'.

She was an early advocate of symbiosis and the case that drew her in was that of lichen. In the late nineteenth century the idea that a plant could be made up of a mutually beneficial union of fungi and algae was the heresy Wakeford refers to, but by the time the idea had been accepted, Beatrix Potter had turned her back on the chauvinistic scientific establishment.

Not content with being a writer and a scientist, she was also a highly regarded painter. Have a look at some of the illustrations in her books. For a start, see Lucie as she climbs over the stile before walking up the hill. Meticulous foxgloves to her left and, to her right, lichens on the drystone wall.

The Tiggy-Winkle fascination extends across the arts. I was interviewed recently for the magazine of the Royal Academy of Dance by someone who wanted to know how similar the character of Mrs T, springing across the stage in the ballet *The Tales of Beatrix Potter*, was to the real beast. It made me think a little more about the problems a hedgehog would face as washer-woman. Apart from the damage caused to the garments from her spines, there is the general aroma of hedgehog that would infuse everything. But still, Potter captured an essential truth about the hedgehog, despite it being utterly preposterous.

Post-Tiggy, the world of children's literature was never the same again. Not just in the volume of anthropomorphic stories, and more specifically hedgehog-related stories, but also in the character given to hedgehogs. Beatrix Potter saw in the hedgehog the epitome of benign. An animal that would not and could not cause harm, but whose quiet industriousness was a quality that should, in fact, be admired. I would be hard pressed to find an ABP hedgehog story that was not kind to the animal.

And there have been so many. The pile I have beside my desk is already considerable. This far from comprehensive gathering contains nineteen picture books, fifteen story books and two wildlife guides.

* * *

One day someone might write a book about the most northerly wildlife hospital I visited. It would feature hedgehogs. A lot. While Andy and Gay Christie, who run Hessilhead, look after far more than our spiky friends, they have been at the centre of efforts to get the cull stopped on the Uists and have hundreds of rescued animals passing through their hands each year.

Beyond Glasgow, near the village of Gateside, there is a rough track off the narrow road. If you did not know, you would not give it a second glance, but at the end of this track there is something miraculous. It is as if Heath Robinson had retired to North Ayrshire and dedicated his remaining days to constructing elaborate techniques of wildlife care out of the most basic ingredients. This is very unlike the modern hospitals of St Tigs and Vale, but it bustles with a healthy energy.

As I arrived the day shift was ending and a steady stream of people were heading for the chalets that are their accommodation. There are qualified vets from Italy and trainees from Spain, England and Scotland. There was a quality in their smiles and chatter that tells a story of hard work done willingly. Gay and Andy were just finishing a round of feeding the young birds and hedgehogs. Some of these animals need to be fed half-hourly during the day; others need to be fed every two hours, all day long. It is obviously very demanding, especially when there is a surge of youngsters in spring.

After a coffee I got a chance to look around the hospital and the convalescence cages. I was keen to meet a famous non-hedgehog guest, simply because it is not every day one gets to play with a fox. Fergus was a delight.

'He is a complete failure,' Gay declared as he wound himself around my legs. 'He came to us from a barbecue. Someone had rescued him when he was young and then released him when he looked big enough. The problem was that he was just too friendly and we were called as he had ended up jumping on to the cook's shoulders.'

Fergus has his uses: he may be a failure as he cannot be released into the wild, but he makes a wonderful advocate for the oft-maligned reynardine. How seductive a tame wild animal can be; despite being an adult, he behaved like a juvenile, submissive and playful.

It all started with a swan. Andy was working as a countryside ranger and would often get handed the odd waif and stray to patch up, but then came a swan. It had swallowed a fishing hook and the vet they took it to said there was nothing to be done without an operation. As Gay and Andy had no money, it was euthanized.

And that changed their lives. In 1970 they reared their first fox cubs and have hardly drawn breath since then. Andy took early retirement in the mid-1990s and Hessilhead has flourished. Now they receive around 3,500 animals a year. And the most popular mammal? No prizes for guessing that it is the hedgehog.

'It was non-stop this spring,' Gay recalled. 'Luckily the hedgehog peak arrived before we started to get really busy with fledglings, but even so we had 100 hedgehogs arrive in just five days, 241 in total.'

That seems like a lot of hedgehogs, but to get

an idea of what it means to an already stretched team of staff and volunteers you just need to do a brief calculation. First thing in the morning the hogs are cleaned out and given fresh bedding, food and water. They are also weighed, so that tabs can be kept on their progress. That all takes an experienced carer about ten minutes per animal, which works out at an extra sixteen hours of work per day arriving in just one week.

As soon as they can get them back out into the wild, they do. But not knowing what happens to them always preys on their minds. 'We cannot afford to radio-track them,' Andy said. 'So it was great to get a call the other day from someone who just said, "I got your number from a hedgehog." And he had seen this hedgehog toddling across his garden accompanied by four babies. What a result.'

This filled my mind with wonderful images of talkative hedgehogs, until Andy burst the fantastical bubble with the explanation: 'This year we tagged each hedgehog with a little plastic marker glued on to the spines. It had a unique number for the hog, so we could track it back to our records, along with our phone number.'

It is this simple pragmatism that makes Gay and Andy so attractive. They are just trying their hardest to do the best for animals that are going to show scant regard for the care they receive. And in some cases, fight quite hard against the care. So why? Why are people willing to invest so much time and energy in such an unreciprocated relationship?

Initially Gay sounded rather soft: 'Well, it's how they look, their twitchy nose and the way they look up at you. It is very appealing.' But she soon brought this down to earth: 'Though they are smelly, they show no affection, no gratitude. And that is part of the reason why they are such good animals to work with for rehabilitation. They don't get tame; they retain their wildness.'

And this is something I can really relate to. Hedgehogs can have a lot done to them, but they remain robustly immune to human interference. There are many people who tell me about their hedgehog, who comes to their garden every night. They even get worried when they go on holiday. Who will feed their hedgehog? Well, hedgehogs are quite adept at fending for themselves and Pat Morris tackled this rather proprietorial notion with a delightfully simple experiment. He got people to put a spot of paint or nail varnish on the spines of their hedgehog and of any other hog that might turn up. Most people found that their hedgehog was in fact many hedgehogs.

However many 'owners' suburban hedgehogs may have, they are still beset by numerous challenges. Gay and Andy have had them come in with all conceivable – and some inconceivable – traumas. Stuck down drains or in septic tanks, or, depressingly, deliberately beaten, kicked or burned. Sometimes it is the simple acts of human carelessness that create the most distressing cases. 'The rubber bands dropped by the postman can be disastrous,' explained Andy. 'We have had hedgehogs that have the bands stuck around their bodies or legs. The bands have been pushed into their flesh, flies have laid eggs and maggots are eating the hedgehogs alive. They are tough, those hedgehogs, and can make a full recovery if we get to them in time.'

Andy is not immune to the charm of the hedgehogs either: 'They are such confident wee animals. Everybody sees them, they don't run away, you can pick them up and get a good look at them. But perhaps the most important thing is that they don't make violent movements. Even a mouse makes sudden darting movements that can scare people, but no one could feel threatened by a hedgehog.'

Andy and Gay had to get back to the hospital for another round of feeding the wee beasties before I joined them for food and some fine whisky. On the way up past the cage of crows, all looking excitedly towards the outside world, seeming to know that their release was imminent, Gay points to the trees that surround this field of sheds and aviaries. 'We rescued them as well,' she exclaims. 'They were along a disused railway line that was about to be converted into a cycle path and would have just been destroyed, so we have rescued them, rehabilitated them and released them into the wild.' She smiles with innocent self-satisfaction.

I really hope that they can one day stand back and look with pride as Hessilhead takes flight, or snuffles off into the undergrowth. Like the animals they care for, the centre has to learn to cope in the wild on its own.

That snuffling — hard to describe, but when you have heard it, it is so distinctive, and by far the easiest way of finding hedgehogs.

When Ted Hughes heard it he was so moved that he wrote not a poem, but a letter to a friend in which he described meeting a hedgehog and deciding to take it home. The great poet realised his companion was suffering in confinement and was moved to kiss away its tears.

On the other side from Ted Hughes is Pam Ayres, who has written a manifesto for hedgehog conservation, one that I think we should take up as an anthem for the BHPS.

In Defence of Hedgehogs

> I am very fond of hedgehogs
> Which makes me want to say,
> That I am struck with wonder,
> How there's any left today,
> For each morning as I travel
> And no short distance that,
> All I see are hedgehogs,
> Squashed. And dead. And flat.

And on it goes for many more verses. Surpassed in length, though, by the imagination of the prolifically inventive Terry Pratchett – 'The Hedgehog Can Never Be Buggered At All'. This song has taken on a life of its own, Pratchett's original was just an idea of what unspeakably rude outpourings may emerge from a drunken witch called Nanny Ogg in the *Wyrd Sisters*; but readers were not content and have created a many-versed investigation into the possibilities of bestiality, returning to the truism about the hedgehogs' impregnable backside.

The Archbishop of Canterbury, Rowan Williams, chose a

rather more sedate ditty for one of his Desert Island Discs, 'The Hedgehog's Song' from the Incredible String Band.

I was lucky enough to have a chat with the song's composer, Mike Heron. Why did he gift a hedgehog with such wisdom? 'I needed to find an animal that would chide me for my lack of commitment in the song and real life as the song is about my relationship with a beautiful French girl.' He then surprised me by revealing that the choice of a hedgehog was arbitrary, especially as it feels so right. 'Well, after I'd written the song, I got to meet many more hedgehogs, and yes, there is something special. There is something about the hedgehog that punches well above its weight.'

Hedgehogs can be woven into many philosophies and my favourite came out of the blue at a party. I met someone who had studied a lot of Buddhism, so much so that she had renamed herself Maitrisara. We exchanged pleasantries and when I said what I was up to I mentioned that people invariably have a hedgehog story to share. She looked a little bewildered, seemingly disproving my point. But a short while later there was a look of complete satisfaction as she said, 'Ah, I had forgotten about the transcendental hedgehog.' Now, that is too good an opener not to get me hooked. 'I had this Buddhist teacher who was trying to explain to us the point of meditation and Buddhist practice. And he hit upon a story to help make it clearer. He pointed to the garden. "Every evening I put out food for the hedgehog," he explained. "Now, putting out food does not mean that I will see a hedgehog and, in the same way, meditating does not mean you will achieve enlightenment. But both will make success more likely." And that was my introduction to the transcendental hedgehog.' And mine as well.

All around the world references to hedgehogs have snuffled into the vernacular. They have been appropriated by every art and craft; used as metaphors in philosophy; they sell us shoes, banking and expensive bondage equipment. But, in this post-Potter world, there is a common theme of gentle compassion.

The hedgehog works because we are drawn to the very idea of what it is to be a hedgehog. Perhaps it is because the hedgehog seems so at home in its skin. Hedgehogs are very happy being hedgehogs. And you can't say that for all animals – when the blackbird flusters away in shock, again, at the sight of her umpteenth unthreatening human, you do begin to wonder how happy she is.

But that does not explain why people so readily dedicate their lives to caring for the little animals.

There are plenty of quite superficial reasons – most focusing on the need to redress the damage done by humanity. We are interfering with nature every time we get into a car. Not just by injuring and killing wildlife on the roads, but by changing the climate with our exhausts. Every time we take a bite of food from the industrial agriculture factory that was once the countryside, we are interfering with the natural world. And every time we take a strimmer thoughtlessly to the undergrowth, or light a bonfire without first checking if it is anybody's home, we are interfering.

But I believe there is a deeper reason. Partly it is 'biophilia', an idea developed by Edward O. Wilson, an astoundingly inventive, clever and knowledgeable Harvard biologist. He asserts that there is an innate need for humanity to have contact with the natural world. But partly I think it is because positive selection for nurturing behaviour among humans is strong. The long-running evolutionary struggle between the need for lengthy gestation to allow all of our amazing faculties to develop and the need for women to be able to walk on two legs (if our heads were any bigger at birth, the female pelvis would have to be redesigned in such a way as to prevent bipedal locomotion) has led to the compromise of a helpless infant that requires prolonged care. Parents who have the skills to successfully care for their infants are more likely to have their genes passed on to the next generation.

Hence the positive selection of nurturing behaviour. There is evidence that early, pre-agricultural humans had pets. These animals, while having some utility, were treated differently to proto-livestock and were obviously valued more highly than other species. It could be argued that they were reducing the sense of isolation that adult humans felt when they no longer had infants to care for. That is, the strength of the innate desire to nurture still needed to be met.

If you compare pet animals to their wild counterparts you will notice that the sacrifice an animal makes in becoming a pet is to be infantilized. Not only does this make a pet more pleasant company, but it also ensures nurturing is required for life.

So, we have a genetic predisposition to nurture. We have an

evolutionary history that suggests a tendency to nurture wild animals and tame them into a state of permanent dependency. Throw into the mix an animal that, in many ways, acts as if it were tame. Hedgehogs do not behave like a wild animal. They do not run away. They do not attack. If they do not roll up instantly, they tend to look up at an approaching human in a vulnerable, throat-exposing way that suggests submission. They allow themselves to be looked after, partly because they do not have the capacity to escape, but also in part because they let it happen.

There is, therefore, a degree of inevitability about hedgehogs becoming the number one cared for wild animal – and it follows, then, that there should be no surprise at what has happened in the USA where this hedgehog-nurturing zeal has erupted into perhaps the world's most counterintuitive pet-keeping craze. Who would have thought that a smelly, grumpy, solitary, nocturnal and spiny animal would sweep a country into a frenzy of pet-hedgehog-keeping?

PART TWO

Obsession

CHAPTER
FIVE

*A Brief Interlude
at the International
Hedgehog Olympic Games*

Buttercup was a strange-looking hedgehog. And not just because she was small, blonde and with the rather prominent ears of an African hedgehog. She had a hump; a little spiny dromedary. She was also a star of the International Hedgehog Olympic Games. Having scored well in the sprint and the hurdles, she was about to reveal her class, matching her physical prowess with the artistic demands of the floor exercises.

Some might find it hard to imagine the IHOG. The (human) Olympic Committee certainly were not so sure and wrote to the (hedgehog) Olympic Committee in 2005, asking that they ensure that no one was under the impression that there was any endorsement on the part of the official (human) body. Having witnessed IHOG in the flesh and the other Olympics on TV, I can assure you that there is no chance for confusion. The contestants are far better-behaved and less involved with performance-enhancing drugs at the IHOG.

Even so, the sexes have to be segregated. Male hedgehogs do everything first and only when they have finished are the females allowed to compete. The reason for this is simple: male hedgehogs are easily distracted. If there is the scent of a female, there is little hope of getting any sense from the male (is this just hedgehogs?).

On the richly patterned carpet in a function room at the Double Tree Hotel, Denver, 5 metres of plastic track had been laid. The crowd of people leaning forward might have been off-putting to less resilient athletes, and to be honest some did end up going in the wrong direction, but Buttercup completed the sprint with determination. Placed in her plastic ball (like a large version of something a hamster might play in) by her owner, Zug Standing Bear, she resolutely followed the track, gaining momentum before rolling off the end to the silent cheers of the excited crowd. (Silent-cheering is a useful technique when in the company of potentially highly strung individuals, and involves waving both hands, if available, vigorously in the air. It was originally developed as a form of sign language for people with hearing difficulties, but works just as well with nervous hedgehogs.)

The hurdles were more of a challenge, requiring a little coercion. Up on stage a row of tables was covered with a 3-metre partitioned run. Each partition had a hole which was incrementally further off the ground than the one preceding it and the hedgehog had to either complete the run in the quickest time or get as far as it could. The owner could encourage, lure and generally persuade the hedgehog that everyone would be happier if it cooperated. The dangling of a mealworm, a small maggoty grub favoured by both hedgehogs and their owners (more on that later), in front of the snout was allowed, but actual contact was forbidden. Buttercup was one of the few to complete the course.

A word of warning: if you want to go and check the results for yourself, IHOG is, confusingly, also the abbreviation for 'interference hedgehog', one of a family of signalling molecules that mediate animal development and is linked to human cancers.

So to the floor exercises. Buttercup was returned to the carpet and placed among the tools of her art. There was a see-saw, a plastic horse, a tunnel, a ball and a mat. Hedgehogs were first placed on the mat and the clock started. They then had two minutes to impress the judge, who was noting both physical abilities and the style with which actions were completed. Walking through the tunnel is great, but it can be done with greater or lesser flair. Sniffing the horse is all well and good, but doing it with some style, that makes a difference. Strategic self-anointing is highly regarded, though defecation is not encouraged. The marking system seems a little esoteric, but after the eighteen contenders had been through their paces, there was no doubting the winner. Buttercup had made her human so proud. As Standing Bear clutched this little rescued hedgehog to his bosom, along with her rosette, I wondered if I could see a little moisture in the corner of his eye.

'I almost fell over when the IHOG Gold Medallist was announced,' he said. 'She stumbled and fell and ran and ran. Her body is tiny and malformed, but she has a heart as big as all outdoors.'

Buttercup is a hedgehog who does not know she is disabled. She was discarded and ended up at Denver Dumb Friends League. She has scoliosis, severe curvature of the spine. When

Standing Bear picked her up, he assumed that she had a tumour on her back, there was such a pronounced hump. And when the X-ray was shown to a vet, he assumed that this must have been taken from a dead animal, the twist was so extreme. But Buttercup was very much alive that night.

Standing Bear was my host for the Rocky Mountain Hedgehog Show, of which the IHOG is a highlight. He runs the Flash and Thelma Memorial Hedgehog Rescue up in Divide, high in the mountains above Colorado Springs, and had inducted me into the arcane world of hedgehog lore before I was thrust into the heaving heart of obsession. I later found that there were only around sixty people (and about 100 hedgehogs) at the show; it certainly felt like a lot more.

Standing Bear's home is amazing. A couple of kilometres from metalled roads, it is so tranquil, sitting on a hill above a small lake, its golden wood glows in the morning sun. Deer and foxes loiter and kingfishers splash into the lake. However, the fairly safe bear made no appearance while I was there.

Standing Bear shares this haven with up to sixty-three hedgehogs and Virginia, his wife. They were amazing hosts, at least Standing Bear and Virginia were, welcoming me like a long-lost friend and turning me into a new-found one. Virginia married young, had three daughters and then reinvented herself by inventing a new discipline that now has international attention, forensic nursing. When I asked if she minded me just getting on with making supper as I was hungry, she illustrated perfectly how distant her previous existence now is. 'I would rather do an autopsy than cook dinner,' she said.

Standing Bear's history is no less remarkable. He started telling me some of it on the ride back from the airport and I really was not sure if he was just pulling my leg. Born into a mixed family, pulling all the best bits from Mohawk, Wampanoag, Scottish and Irish ancestors, he joined the army and made his way up the ranks in the Military Police, working in Germany, where he learned an awful lot about wine (he has a cellar of stunning bottles, the 1945 Baron Rothschild, complete with V label, must be among his most prized possessions). In Russia he shared a flat with Shostakovich, giving him a life-long love of classical music, before being sent to Vietnam to investigate war crimes committed by his own side. This was the beginning of his great change, when the appalling behaviour of some of his own men made him question whether he was in this fight on the right side. 'I talked to the Vietcong,' he explained. 'They just wanted to be able to grow enough rice to feed their children.'

After Vietnam, Standing Bear returned to his people and herded sheep with the Navajo, spending time with the medicine men and women before becoming involved with a land-rights struggle. But the military were not finished with him and, thanks to a stint as a bodyguard to President Gerald Ford, he ended up with a series of commissions, rising to the rank of major-general, before finally giving it up and focusing his energies on teaching investigation and forensics.

So it was obvious that Standing Bear was destined for a life with hedgehogs.

'It was Virginia's fault,' he explained. 'Back in 1993 she saw one in a shop and brought it home with her – that was Flash. The deal was that she would take him with her, and she did, tucking him into a pocket as she got on to planes, keeping him quiet during lectures.'

But as her career advanced, so did the calls for her to travel further afield. Standing Bear had to look after Flash. And then there was the first rescue. 'Usual story,' he said. 'A student was off to join the Peace Corps, forgetting that they had a responsibility back here, so I took Thelma in and that was the beginning of it all. And it would have been churlish to turn down the next one, who inevitably became known as Louise, as they were two darn independent ladies.'

How did someone who was exposed to some of the worst aspects of humanity in Vietnam end up like this? 'Well, you can either harden your heart or learn lessons,' he explained. And it is not as if hedgehogs were the beginning of it all; he had already been involved in wolf rescue – which seems, somehow, more in keeping.

Ironically, Virginia feels she has lost her husband to hedgehogs – though as he points out, he doesn't play golf, and that would have been far worse. And while she may fume about the time he spends clearing out the large Perspex boxes that are the home of the rescued hogs, she has also seen a hedgehog, Little Flash, become an informal mascot of the Colorado Chapter of the International Association of Forensic Nurses. 'Many of my colleagues,' Virginia said, 'are sexual assault examiners. To help pull ourselves from the bleakness that this view of life can present I pointed out that the hedgehog is a great symbol, a female hedgehog cannot be sexually assaulted.'

My invitation to Colorado followed a meeting of the European Hedgehog Research Group in Germany. One of the contributors was Donnasue Graesser from Yale, who had been looking at heritable problems facing hedgehogs. She persuaded the Hedgehog Welfare Society of the United States to fly me over for the Colorado show in Denver in 2007. Organized in conjunction with the International Hedgehog Association, this is the biggest event in the hedgehog calendar.

I was flattered to be invited, but a little daunted. The nearest I had come to a pet hedgehog was in the care of Janis just outside Blackpool, and that was grumpy. Yet I really wanted to find out what was behind it all. Why were people so keen to make a pet of a hedgehog? I have been a hedgehog lover for many years, but have never wanted to change the relationship to one of domestication. In fact, part of what I love so much about hedgehogs is their wildness. Others have written eloquently about the wildness of place – landscape that is 'will'd', still retaining its will. Well, that is something so true about the hedgehog; it is a self-willed little animal. And, more importantly, they smell.

To help me get to the bottom of the obsession I joined Standing Bear as he cleaned out the hedgehogs. There is a sizeable and well-heated shed that houses the bulk of the rescued animals; even when the snow lies thick outside, the hedgehogs need to be kept between 18 and 27 degrees centigrade. A few others are in the more intensive-care area abutting his office. The hedgehogs either share or have their own 'condo' – a wooden enclosure or plastic tub containing a few essentials: water, food, a shelter made from the bark of half a tree trunk, a fleece blanket and a wheel.

The wheels, which many hedgehogs seem to adore, are glorified hamster wheels, 30 centimetres in diameter, and are the subject of many intense engineering debates. There are some commercially available and there are still attempts being made to perfect the design. The design has to take into consideration the fact that while the hedgehogs like to run, they are not as sure-footed as more conventional wheel-runners, such as rodents. 'Perhaps that is why people like them so much,' Standing Bear muses. 'They are just a bit bumbling and clumsy, like us humans.' Still, some hedgies will run for hours at night. I did suggest that this energy could be utilized, perhaps they could help light the hospital.

Standing Bear introduced me to some of his favourite charges. This is where I first met the improbably athletic Buttercup and got to see the X-ray that clearly shows her meandering spine. Then there were Fred and Wilma. Both now over four years old, they arrived in an appalling condition from California, each with a gangrenous leg.

Standing Bear explained that hedgehogs are illegal in California, and around the United States there is considerable disunity with regards to hedgehogs, with seven states outlawing the prickly beasts. California apparently bans anything exotic, apart from the people, that is. The state is understandably protective of its agriculture – which happens to be made up of largely introduced species. They have labelled African hedge-hogs with a 'D', for detrimental. And it would not be hard to imagine domestic hedgehogs 'going wild'. Similarly in Arizona, the environment is not too different from their central African home. Hawaii, too, is understandable, with so much biodiversity being destroyed by various immigrants. But Maine and Vermont remain a bit of a mystery, while Pennsylvania's legislation is so complex that anything could be deemed illegal and they have even executed possession orders to seize these inoffensive critters. Standing Bear then pauses, spits an imaginary plug of tobacco and slips into a remarkable impression of a county sheriff from Georgia: 'We've had it with all these exotic species coming here and raising Cain.' But as Standing Bear points out, Georgia's problems are almost exclusively insect-based. Perhaps a few more insectivores would be useful.

Lucky flying hedgehogs can travel up front with a human – though they must be confined within a container that will sit under the seat in front and need their own ticket (interna-tional travel is a problem because the passport photographs all look so alike to humans). But not all airlines are happy, only allowing dogs and cats to travel this way. One passenger got her hedgehog on board by calling her a 'Tasmanian quilled cat'. Thank goodness for the limited scope of zoology lessons in some American classrooms.

If the hedgehog is not allowed in the cabin, or is travelling solo, then they have to be put in with the freight and need a veterinary health certificate. Most of Standing Bear's hedgehogs arrive this way and he is on first-name terms with the folk at the Frontier Airlines Air Freight terminal.

The vet gave Fred and Wilma little hope, but also thought that the legs looked like they would not need amputation, as they would drop off on their own accord. Which they did. And now they have a special place at the rescue. 'Wilma is my chief petting hedgehog,' Standing Bear explained. 'I can line up forty children at a school and she will jump forty times, each time she is touched, and this will cause each of the forty children to jump as well. And they will remember the first time they met a hedgehog.

'And this is Pepper,' he said. 'Now she is a strange one.' Standing Bear put on a hairdryer (it is the easiest way to dry a hedgehog) and Pepper emerged sharply from the little fleece bag in which he sleeps, ran to his water dish and sat in it. 'You see that? Every time I put this on – or the vacuum cleaner – he jumps into the water. I think he thinks the noise is a threat to his water.'

Earlier in the year Pepper stopped rushing out to protect the water and Standing Bear was concerned. Sudden changes in behaviour can indicate that something is not quite right with the animal. But as closely as he checked, he could find nothing wrong, until he noticed Pepper was in a very slightly different fleece sleeping bag from normal. And as soon as he was returned to his usual bag, he returned to his water-protecting duties. Standing Bear is convinced Pepper was on strike, offended by the change in circumstances.

Over a glass of very fine Riesling that night Standing Bear reminisced about the hedgehogs that have asserted their personality so strongly on his life. He has invented an entire mythology about them, stimulated by his military heritage; many hedgehogs receive ranks, promotion and commendation. He has even written a book set in a hedgehog world. It is the first of the Hedgehog Chronicles, *The Gathering: Secretly Saving the World.*

Apparently the hedgehog characters first hit him when he went to an airport to rendezvous with a woman who had been given an ultimatum by her fiancé – me or the hedgehog – and was handing Spiker into the custody of Standing Bear. Spiker made a bid for freedom and took refuge under a ticket counter at Dallas airport. His grumpy disposition coupled with his creative escape attempts put Standing Bear in mind of a marine major-general he had met, so that was the beginning of that world.

My favourite story, however, was of Critical Bill. He was dropped from a passing car on to a school playground in Fort Collins, northern Colorado. As the car drove off, two inquisitive children approached and saw a ball of spines. Being responsible, they went off in search of a teacher, who was naive in the ways of the hedgehog and was alarmed by the hissing and spitting noise emanating from the impenetrable bundle, so went and retrieved the Principal, who was also perplexed, until the noise started again, at which point he dialled 911 and was put through to Hazardous Materials Emergency – HAZMAT – who set in motion a complete emergency response that included commandeering a cement lorry. The plan being to empty the contents over the suspect device that had the experienced army folk scratching their heads.

The responsibility to take a closer look fell to supervisor Tom Buckleton, who crouched behind his shrapnel shield as the cement lorry approached. Twenty-five years with Army Explosive Ordnance Disposal units and he had never seen anything like this. But then something even more surprising happened. With the lorry came some very welcome shade for the ball of prickles and Bill the hedgehog relaxed, lifted himself up and extended a tentative snout into the shade. Tom Buckleton almost fainted as he saw the bomb grow legs and a nose, and that is how Critical Bill was named.

Throughout my time with hedgehogs it has become obvious that they are blessed with great character and these pets are no different. But I was still to be convinced about the general petability of the animals.

There was a room full of people in Denver ready to try to make me see the light, so Standing Bear and I packed up a carload of hedgehogs – ten of them in travel boxes across the back seats of his car. And not just any old car; for some reason Standing Bear has a fondness for very well-protected cars and this one weighs almost 3 tonnes and comes with a 'class 2 protection package' – which apparently means it is bulletproof. It used to belong to an (obviously nervous) diplomat.

We made it to the Double Tree Hotel in Denver just in time for Standing Bear to register his entrants in the show and prepare Buttercup for Olympic triumph. The obvious question here is, where did these hedgehogs come from? There are no native American hedgehogs. Despite flourishing there in the Miocene, they have been absent for around 5 million years.

There was a man in Nigeria who was involved in the export of exotic animals to the pet trade, mostly reptiles. In 1991 he was approached by some people who happened to have a crate full of hedgehogs. They claimed that their area was being overrun with starving hedgehogs and they were doing them a favour by finding them a new home. The man thought they looked cute and reckoned that other people might think so too, so he bought them at fifty cents a piece and shipped all 2,000 of them to New York. Where they sold, fast, through the wholesale trade – on to pet shops all over the country.

He kept buying all the hedgehogs he could get his hands on. Two species were coming to him, *Atelerix albiventris* and *Atelerix algirus* (*Atelerix* is a genus of hedgehogs made up of four species all found in Africa). The names are easy translations – the white-bellied, also known as the central African, and the Algerian hedgehogs. Quickly they became the latest must-have pet. He exported around 50,000 to the United States and reckons another 30,000 came from other distributors before the import of all wild animals from countries with Hoof and Mouth Disease was banned in 1994.

By that time hedgehogs had become a fad pet; a lot of money was being made. Even the support organizations were in on the capitalization of this little animal. 'Your best returns are with the North American Hedgehog Association,' trumpeted a leaflet.

The *Washington Post* headlined an article in August 1994 'Going Hedgehog Wild – the Latest, Not Always Legal, Fashion Pet' and went on to give an idea of the economics – and how swiftly they change. A pet shop in Washington, DC, said they were selling about six a month at $188 – but that only a few months earlier they were fetching $500. This was a result of fading faddism coupled with increased supply from breeders. In fact, the paper had missed the peak. A year earlier there had been reports of breeding pairs selling for $4,500, and one 'snowflake' pair going for $5,500.

There is still a trade in hedgehogs, but it is on a much smaller scale and great riches are not to be gained. For example, it is possible to buy a quality hog from a reputable breeder for $150–$225, complete with 24/7 support and even, in some cases, free 'baby-sitting' for when the owner needs a holiday. And they have recently made an appearance in the UK, with headlines in May 2008 extolling the virtues of this 'must-have pet'. Perhaps there will be another boom and bust here? If so the consequences could be serious, as unscrupulous (or dim) traders might try to pass off our resident hogs as African pets. And the very presence of a native hedgehog population will make the task of discarding an unwanted pet all the easier to stomach.

At least the US pet hedgehog fad did not go the way of Vietnamese potbellied pigs, which once sold for thousands of dollars, until the craze passed and they were being given away for free. I put this down to a slow emergence of common sense. 'A pig is a pig is a pig . . . Keeping them in a house is next to impossible,' explained the Humane Society.

The extreme figures being paid for hedgehogs help to explain what I uncovered when I started looking into this back in the UK. So keen were people to get their hands on these animals that at least two attempts were made to get hold of hedgehogs from England. Now, whether this was someone ignorant of the differences between the African species and our own, I don't know; because I would really not be interested in spending too long too close to our beloved Tiggy in captivity.

The two species that formed the basis of the US breeding stock have evolved a highly efficient strategy for coping with times when water is scarce. They do not waste water, absorbing as much as possible from their food as it passes through their intestines. Our hedgehogs, on the other hand, come from a much wetter environment and as such can be more casual about the amount of water they absorb. The significance of that physiological insight is that our hedgehogs tend to have wetter and smellier faeces.

I am not sure how malleable our hedgehogs are either. While there are a few stories of hedgehogs becoming tame, I find it hard to imagine any of the ones I have worked with sitting quite so comfortably in the hands and pockets of adoring people. Though there were a couple of stories reported by the British nineteenth-century naturalist John Wood. In his 1870 publication, *Natural History Rambles: Lane and Field*, he states, 'It can be easily tamed, and is a great help in houses which are much infested with cockroaches. Being nocturnal in its habits like the cockroaches, it makes great havoc with them at night, and really needs little other food.'

And in his 1903 book, *Petland Revisited*, he relates this remarkable tale of tameness. The hedgehog would

> run around the table, stopping before each person, and asking to be fed. If refused, he used to frown ... and with an angry snort he would pass on to the next person.
>
> One day his sensitive nostrils detected an unknown scent. He quested about until he discovered a tumbler filled with hot negus.* Some of it was offered to him in a spoon, and he took to it so kindly that before long he could not walk, and I had to carry him to bed. Next day, when some negus was offered to him, he refused it indignantly.

Though alcohol wasn't available for the contestants at IHOG, I was intrigued to find that hedgehog massage was on offer. This must be one of the greatest challenges facing a masseuse. How

---

* From Mrs Beeton's drinks recipes: 'To make Negus – to every pint of port wine allow 1 quart of boiling water, 1/4 lb of sugar, 1 lemon, grated nutmeg to taste.' This was a drink served at children's parties ... and I thought giving them fizzy drinks was dodgy.

do you massage a hedgehog? There is a whole series of strokes that Vicky McLean from Oregon is convinced improve the quality of life of the recipients. Effleurage, pettrissage, pincer palpation, passive stretch, friction and hydrotherapy all play a part, just as they do in human encounters. The combination of stroking, stretching, pressing and rubbing helps to relieve the stiffness that occurs in debilitated hogs.

Another technique that has been used with apparent success by vet Priscilla Dressen is acupuncture. I would really like to see a photograph of that in action – let the prickler be prickled.

The Official Booklet of Standards for showing hedgehogs dictates what is a perfect-looking hedgehog and presents an almost sinister eugenicist vision:

> Hedgehogs are cute, friendly and have an appeal that is truly unique. However, they do have certain physical characteristics that can be improved upon. As an example, being an insectivore, there is a natural tendency for them to have narrow heads and faces. By widening the head and shortening the face, the rest of the body will naturally follow. The animal's stance will widen ... This will create a far more attractive animal that should, theoretically, have the capacity to birth larger litters.

The standards also define the appearance of hedgehogs, splitting them into seven classes. The International Hedgehog Association describes these as: standard (grey-ish), apricot (pale with hint of orangey-beige), snowflake (a dusting of white spines among pale banded spines), white, albino, pinto (piebald) and AOC (any other colours). A bit like a paint chart, but harder to apply to the wall.

And then the competition began. Owners took their charges up on to the stage and placed them on tables, facing the audience. The judge spent considerable time assessing the qualities of each hedgehog – how do they match up to the exacting standards laid down by the IHA? Points are given for the quality of body shape ('the rump is to be spherical over the top with a straight drop to the skirt'); weight ('obese animals will be disqualified'); colour; ears ('to be large and well spaced'); face ('shall proceed from the quill line to the nose in as straight a line as possible') and temperament.

It is the last of these that proved my downfall when I got roped into helping out showing a hedgehog. The adult female pinto category had just two entries, both owned by a breeder called Floyd. One was a sure winner; the other was handed to me. Apparently it is better to win by merit rather than by being the sole contender. So I was given Katrina. I felt that something was not right – everyone else seemed to have hedgehogs that lay calmly in their hands, or would actively enjoy a little tummy tickle. Katrina fizzed like a cartoon bomb, ready to explode. And in case I had not got the message, she persisted in little jumps, trying to impale her spines into my hand. I placed her carefully on the table in front of a room full of grinning spectators. Floyd's little girl was being cute and charming. Katrina resolutely refused to unroll and the judge looked at me rather pityingly.

Needless to say, we lost. Seems like the audience was in on the joke, though, getting the Brit up on stage with the grumpiest hedgehog in the USA. Perhaps that is why I still failed to 'get it' – I could not see the attraction. Are they trying to create a new domesticated species or breed wild hedgehogs with accommodating personalities? I like my hedgehogs wild, grumpy and outdoors.

But attraction there is and it bites deep. In fact, it seems to have a more powerful hold on people than more obviously charismatic pets, such as dogs. Owners talked about how they had pets of many species but had never felt as passionate as they did about hedgehogs. I certainly found, from talking to a lot of people at the show, that hedgehogs have a distinct practical advantage over many other pets – very few people express any allergies to hedgehogs. People who have craved pets but been unable to tolerate all manner of animals seem able to live with a hedgehog. Additionally, they are small and undemanding. Apparently there are many people who are unable to attend the show because of infirmity and hedgehogs are just the perfect pet for them. They do not need walking; they are happy to run on a wheel and are also, as I saw, happy to display behaviour that is interpretable as affection. They will snuggle up into nooks and corners, armpits and pockets, and remain relaxed in the company of familiar people.

Eventually there had to be a winner. Or more accurately, two winners, as there is a tradition of holding two shows, one in the morning and one in the afternoon. For the record, the winners of the Rocky Mountain Hedgehog Show 2007 were:

Morning
Grand Champion: Ying Yang (Floyd Aprill)
Reserve Grand Champion: Showtyme aka 'Brenda's Pinto'
(Brenda Sandoval)

Afternoon
Grand Champion: Bindi Sue (Pat Storm)
Reserve Grand Champion: Fannie Mae (Frances and
Andrew Beamon)

The excitement of the announcement of the grand champion over, there could have been an anticlimax, but there was the banquet to look forward to. Much more than just a meal, this has become a ritual in hedgehogging circles.

After eating, and just before the solemn playing of 'The Music of the Night' from *Phantom of the Opera* (an important component of the ceremony; a paean to nocturnal life), someone was busily putting boxes of paper tissues on all the tables. I really thought we were going to be in for a little of the sorts of tears that accompany Charles Dibdin's 'Tom Bowling' every year at the Last Night of the Proms – that is, tears with the tongue stuffed firmly into the cheek, while clutching at the provided handkerchiefs.

Then came the evening's speaker, Dawn Wrobel. Dawn has been a leading breeder of hedgehogs, but has redefined herself as an animal communicator. And it was in that capacity she was speaking.

She explained how we all have the capacity to speak to animals

– well, I knew that. We used to have a dog, a beautiful Labrador called Brandy. I could speak to him for hours. Out in the Welsh hills I would say, 'Come here, Brandy,' many, many times, but he never listened. Apparently I was missing the point a little. Dawn believes that we all have an ability to communicate telepathically with animals.

To work out what she should say at the show, she had gone to her hedgehog matriarch – Sweet Blessing – and asked her for advice. The message was simple: 'Just go and ask the other hedgehogs what they would like to say to their people.' And that is what Dawn gave us, a series of greetings from the spiky companions of many of the people in the room.

'Don't sweat the small stuff,' said Greta. 'Don't be afraid to try something new,' said Munchkin. 'More sex,' was the blunt request from Aldebaron. Keiki wanted to be 'upside down; sometimes you need to get a different view'. Sweet Blessing concluded this portion of the event by saying we should all 'worry less, lighten up, challenge yourselves and have more fun'.

What are they feeding their hedgehogs? Fortune cookies?

Later I chatted with Dawn. She began by explaining how the pet-keeping craze started, and had a wonderful theory. 'Initially people who had hedgehogs were computer geeks,' she explained. 'People who were up all night and just a bit strange wanted a pet like them – prickly exterior, soft interior. I should know; I was a computer geek.'

Dawn describes herself as 'clairaudient', which means she can talk to and hear hedgehogs. And she is not alone. There is a thriving industry of animal communicators, pet psychics who can find out why Flopsy rabbit is so grumpy or how Rover is coping with his death. If you are an animal communicator you can list yourself on the animaltalk.net website for $100 a year, and there are hundreds who do. I randomly picked a few – you can get a telephone consultation for $45 an hour. Another offers the Healthy Pet, Happy Home Program for just $40 a month for twelve months. To get trained up as a communicator there is a series of courses you can take – and I had a look at one set of options. I have missed out many of the sessions, but this is clearly not something to enter into on a whim:

> Advanced 3, fee: $550
> Advanced 5, fee: $1,100
> Advanced 8, fee: $1,200

And these do not include accommodation, but often have a requirement that you have undertaken the other stages before you can progress to the next. The final three courses are essentially permissions to teach the first three courses – creating quite a nice little cycle.

Dawn describes how she can use the information given to her by a hedgehog to then get a vet to help treat them better. Apparently it is just like ESP. She has communicated with a lot of different species but 'hedgehogs really take on a lot for their owners. They are also the ones most likely to hang around after they die and come back as a hedgehog ghost.'

I had overheard Dawn at the show as she described what she

had been told by a particular hedgehog. She explained to the owners that part of the trouble the couple were having with their hedgehog came from the visits of their last hedgehog, who returns and sits beside her and tells her how he was always jealous of the attention the cat received.

Dawn has delved further into hedgehog awareness and reports that they 'call themselves "star children". They think they came from the stars – I don't know where it came from and it doesn't make sense to those of us here, but it is a common view among hedgehogs that they are a very ancient being. So that is why they choose the people they do to get good care and continue the line.'

I would hate it if people thought I was not an open-minded sort, I really like to think I am, but I did once see some graffiti that seems appropriate: 'Be open-minded, but not so open that your brain falls out.'

And then came the Rainbow Bridge Ceremony.

There is a problem. Pet hedgehogs have a bad habit of starting to wobble, gradually losing motor function until they die. Wobbly Hedgehog Syndrome may sound like a joke, but the results are horrible. No hedgehog has survived WHS, which acts a little like multiple sclerosis, and it seems to be almost entirely restricted to pet hedgehogs in America.

It first emerged soon after the import of hedgehogs was prohibited and has now been identified as an inherited condition, amplified by avaricious breeding. Money was being raised at this event to help find a cure and you could buy a purple and green ribbon to show how much you cared. But there is an additional problem.

A key characteristic for a successful 'show hedgehog' is a calm temperament. Now, it is not natural for a hedgehog to be calm at a hedgehog show – trust me, I was there and it is not even natural for a human to be calm at such an event. Any self-respecting wild animal is going to want to hide away from the smells, noise and lights. Perhaps they might have become accustomed to being handled by one person, but to then tolerate a stranger peering up their rear end ... would you like that?

Winning hedgehogs are calm, unwild and, it now seems, exhibiting a common feature of WHS, as it is always the calm ones that are struck down with the disease. So the desire to breed the wildness out of the hedgehog is perpetuating a miserable condition. Of course, hedgehogs are not alone in this. The desire to create a more servile-looking German shepherd dog resulted in the selection for hip dysplasia.

But none of that mattered as the lights dimmed. The Rainbow Bridge Ceremony is a time when the many hedgehog lovers who have lost their loved ones, their little kids, as many were prone to calling them, get a chance to share their very real grief.

Though I did not know that as it began and was surprised by the palpable shift in the atmosphere. People were reaching for tissues, shifting closer to friends, steeling themselves.

The projector was ready, lights dimmed and emotional Muzak commenced. First there was a short introduction that set the tone for the next twenty minutes:

Just this side of heaven is a place called Rainbow Bridge.

When an animal dies that has been especially close to someone here, that pet goes to Rainbow Bridge.

There are meadows and hills for all of our special friends so they can run and play together.

There is plenty of food, water and sunshine, and our friends are warm and comfortable.

All the animals who had been ill and old are restored to health and vigor; those who were hurt or maimed are made whole and strong again, just as we remember them in our dreams of days and times gone by.

The animals are happy and content, except for one small thing; they each miss someone very special to them, who had to be left behind.

They all run and play together, but the day comes when one suddenly stops and looks into the distance. His bright eyes are intent; his eager body quivers. Suddenly he begins to run from the group, flying over the green grass, his legs carrying him faster and faster.

You have been spotted, and when you and your special friend finally meet, you cling together in joyous reunion, never to be parted again. The happy kisses rain upon your face; your hands again caress the beloved head, and you look once more into the trusting eyes of your pet, so long gone from your life but never absent from your heart.

Then you cross Rainbow Bridge together . . .

As the ceremony – well, I use the word lightly, it was a Powerpoint presentation – continued, I watched all around me crumple into tears. Picture followed picture of hedgehogs who have departed in the two years since the last meeting. With each picture are a few words about the character of the animal and details of the carer. Sometimes a particular image would cause a gasp of sobbing from somewhere in the room and you knew who had lost that hedgehog.

By the end there was just one pair of dry eyes in the house – mine. I was amazed, and slightly jealous of not being able to join in the great exuberance of grief. I have never seen the likes of this for other animals. People talked more passionately about the bond with hedgehogs than they did about their own family members.

One of the purposes of the hedgehog show is to raise money for a number of rescue centres, including the one run by Standing Bear. And a big feature of the evening is the auction. Hedgehoggery is on offer in all its forms: model hedgehogs with acupuncture needles as spines, books and a large patchwork quilt. Hundreds of dollars are raised from some wonderful, and some less wonderful, material.

The atmosphere changed as a call went up to 'get out the worms'.

Brenda, a breeder who runs Heaven Sent Hedgehogs, was busy with some tubes. I looked closer. They were about 15 centimetres long and half filled with green jelly. Someone said something about 'jello shots', but I was none the wiser. Then I saw what she was putting into the tubes. Wriggling on top of the green jelly was a mass of maggots. And shouts went out – 'How much am I bid? How much to see Brenda eat the worms?' Money started to flow forward as the recently sobbing crowd rallied into a baying throng – 'Eat the worms, eat the worms.'

Brenda flamboyantly raised a tube so the crowd could see the contents – the bidding was over $100 already. She put one end of the tube into her mouth, beckoned forth a volunteer who took the other end in his mouth and gave a hard blow, expelling jelly (turns out it is tequila jelly) and maggots into the victim.

Then the odd voice started saying, 'What about Hugh?' – and others joined them. I am sure I could have raised quite a merry penny for hedgehog rescuers across the USA, but maggots? Even though they call them worms, they are mealworms and they look like maggots. Actually, would it make a difference if they were worms? My sister ate worms when young, but I have not eaten any meat in over twenty years and I wasn't about to start with wriggling maggots – never mind how many hedgehogs I might have saved. Oh, and then I found that the jelly was made with gelatine, so I was provided with plenty of excuses.

Jennifer, editor of the Hedgehog Welfare Society's newsletter, grabbed a handful and was disappointed to only get an offer of $40, but wolfed them down anyway – and she did it again later when she found that her exploits had not been caught on camera. The evening felt like anarchy was about to break out, but order was restored by a wonderfully talented band, Dakota Blond, who provided a couple of hours of top-quality entertainment, though I must apologize for missing a chunk in the middle as I was recruited to join a beer run (the hotel's provision was rather pricey).

A group of five of us bundled out of the main door to be

met by heavy rain. I was just following the pack, so we ended up in someone's car for the lengthy drive to the other side of the road . . . apparently this is a fairly typical American response to a problem. After the music we retired to the hospitality suite with our collection of local micro-brews and had a wonderful evening during which I learned much, much that can probably not make it into the book, but suffice it to say there is a porn star nicknamed 'The Hedgehog'.

CHAPTER
SIX

———◆❖◆———

*Hugh's
Hedgehog*

It has long been a fantasy of mine – to embark on a quest to find all fourteen species of spiny hedgehog and possibly even keep a look out for the pretenders, the gymnures and moonrats. This multi-continent mission would take me from my home to the eastern and southern limits of Eurasia and down to the tail of Africa – an Old World quest for an ancient animal.

But in 2007 I was happy to settle for a slightly less extravagant expedition – a search for the bleeding obvious.

A hedgehog called Hugh; a hedgehog about which almost nothing is known. The International Union for Conservation of Nature lists *Hemiechinus hughi* as 'vulnerable'. This means that it faces a high risk of extinction in the wild in the medium term. They believe its habitat in China is severely fragmented, something that seems all too common for our spiny friends.

The idea had loitered around for a while. I searched for more information but found nothing; not even a photograph of *hughi*. The closest I got was the website of Belle & Dean, producers of organic clothes for children. Amazingly, founder and illustrator, Issy, had come across a reference to Hugh's hedgehog and created a hedgehog print that adorns Babygros and T-shirts.

I began to feel a need, a need that transcended logic, to find this hedgehog and photograph my namesake before it vanished for good. And from a purely personal point of view, I wanted to know who was the Hugh after whom it was named.

I began to daydream about donning a leather jacket and battered trilby and heading off on a 1930s-style expedition. Somewhere between the drama of *Indiana Jones* and the passion of *The English Patient* – I was the explorer, dusty, tired yet dashingly rugged. A canvas bag over my shoulder would contain a historic notebook filled with great thoughts, witty quotes (probably in Latin) and immaculate sketches. Possibly there would be a conflict with an evil hedgehog collector.

When I first mentioned my idea of going to China to find *hughi*, Pat Morris laughed: 'No one will take you seriously again.' I had to remind him that actually there were precious few who did, so I was not too worried about that.

What an absurd adventure. When I sat down to plan it, taking into consideration time, money and language, it began to look just a little more complicated. I made a great breakthrough early on by finding Professor Wang Song, mammal expert at the Institute of Zoology in Beijing. Not only did I find him, but he also responded immediately to my email of introduction. He pointed me towards the Natural History Museum in London; he had heard they had a specimen.

The curatorial staff at the South Kensington museum are amazing. Their world mixes the Victorian with the modern. Computer databases quickly link up items that would have taken hours to research, while the workstations are wreathed in the musty smell of old leather-bound books. A perfect match. I began in the library. The snippets of information I had found along the way gave a reference to the first mention of *hughi* in a paper presented by Michael Rogers Oldfield Thomas in 1908.

Oldfield Thomas, as he was known to all, worked his way up the ranks of the Natural History Museum, from clerk to foremost collector. In his time he managed to increase enormously the number of mammal specimens held by the museum, employing collectors around the world. He also named over 2,000 new species before his retirement in 1923. In a poignant conclusion to his personal history, just a few months after the death of his beloved wife he took his own life, acknowledging that he could not manage without her.

The paper was published in the *Proceedings of the General Meetings for Scientific Business of the Zoological Society of London*:

A very dark-coloured, finely speckled species, quite unlike any of the other Chinese hedgehogs. Spines light basally as in *E. miodon*, but the dark ring is much broader, and is followed by quite a narrow light ring, only about 0.5 to 0.8 mm. in length, the point for about the same length is again dark. As a result the whole animal is very dark with a fine whitish ticking, and has quite a different appearance to the broadly washed whitish of the other species. Head, limbs, and belly brown.

Hind foot of type 38 mm.

Hab[itat]. Paochi, Shen-si.

Type [specimen]. Adult female. B.M. No. 0.6.27.2. Presented and collected by Father Hugh.

And there it was, the first reference to the Hugh in question. Further digging revealed a Father Hugh at the Catholic Mission in Hankow, China, who supplied many species to Oldfield Thomas, including ninety-four species of bird from the province of 'Shen-si'. The librarians dug up a magical tome for me. Sometimes I find that books can convey so much more than just the information they contain and this was a case in point. It was a bound collection of letters to Oldfield Thomas, an amazing insight into the life of a naturalist at the turn of the last century.

There was something very sad about the library. I asked what they were doing with the change to electronic communication, as the archive I had my hands on was such an invaluable source of information. There was a pause and then the awful truth came out. The library has not had a budget to even file the correspondence arriving since 1999.

Sitting in the library, locked away from the hubbub of the busy museum corridors, the great tragedy this short-sighted economy represents became clear. We could be living in a new 'dark age'. Future generations may look back at now and wonder what on earth happened, as there are no records to indicate the amazing achievements and accumulations of knowledge.

But I had my hands on the very letters that had been written to Oldfield Thomas. The crisp leaves of autumnal paper, patterned with many rhythmic hands, spoke directly to me from the past:

5th November 1906

My dear Thomas,

My Hungarian friends seem indefatigable and are determined to establish the identity of their flying mice.

With this letter I am sending you per messenger two other kinds of mice. Both of them have been injected with formalin. Will you kindly let me know what they are? The one with the black stripe down the back is a most delightful animal to the uninitiated and I should be very glad if it turned out to be new, and so would my correspondents.

This is really a case of 'reflected glory'; you have inspired me with mouse love and I seem to have infected them.

With kindest regards
Yours very sincerely
N C Rothschild

Unfortunately the letter that had accompanied the specimen of *hughi* was not to be found, but I did find another letter from Father Hugh, dated 18 February 1899, in which he apologizes for the poor quality of specimens he is able to furnish the museum with and complains bitterly about the difficulty of acquiring traps or ammunition for his guns. The scratchy paper was so thin, like the tracing paper the sadists at my prep school placed in the lavatories, that it was a wonder it had lasted so long. But now it was safe (my hands had been swabbed with alcohol to remove traces of fat that could damage the paper before I was allowed anywhere near the pages).

After I had finished with the letters to Oldfield Thomas I was handed a small pile of books that referred to my hedgehog (I was beginning to feel quite proprietorial). It was disturbingly small, but there was one map in *The Mammals of China* that revealed areas where the hedgehog had been seen. Oh my, so few sightings in a country so large. Just twelve dots on the map and each dot, all I had to go on, covered around 1,200 square kilometres, not that far off the area of Greater London. It made me realize that just turning up and going for a wander was not the way to proceed. There was a small cluster around Xi'an and then a lone sighting in Anhui Province. The map also showed the distribution of *Hemiechinus dauricus*, the Daurian hedgehog, further to the north, suggesting that there was not a great crossover. Another map gave the details of sightings of *Hemiechinus auritus*, a long-eared desert hog from the north and west of the country, again quite distant from sightings of *hughi*. However, there was still the chance of meeting unexpected hedgehogs, so the next task was to make sure I knew what *hughi* looked like.

The text gave some hints, the most obvious being the dark tips to the spines. But I needed to have a look and amazingly, deep in the bowels of the museum, there was the original specimen handed to Oldfield Thomas by Father Hugh. Curator Daphne Hills led me by regiments of cabinets, past people peering through microscopes at preserved pieces of beasts. The air hung heavy with the scent of stuffed animals, just how a collection is supposed to smell.

We opened up a cabinet in the far corner and Daphne pulled out a heavy drawer. There were four stiff figures, straight from a hedgehog zombie movie – eyes replaced with cotton wool. There were three species – *Hemiechinus auritus, Hemiechinus dauricus* and *Hemiechinus hughi*. Wearing gloves, she transferred them all to a tray. I had to wait a little longer before I could get my hands on *hughi* as we meandered back through the cabinets to a quiet corner where we could be alone, become better acquainted and get on first-name terms.

What did I learn from this encounter? What did that dried-up corpse tell me? At least it was slightly better stuffed than some of the other examples I had glimpsed in the cabinet.

Carefully I picked up *hughi*. And with good reason did I treat him with reverence. OK, her. That'll teach me to make assumptions, just because she had the name Hugh. The reverence was due to the fact that she was a 'type' specimen. She was the one that defined a new species. When Oldfield Thomas published his paper in 1908, it was based on this very animal.

That is quite an honour. But also rather disturbing. As I looked closely at her, the only defining feature I could make out was the distinctively dark-tipped spines. While I have never met a hedgehog looking like her, I have met hedgehogs with widely differing spine colours. Could *hughi* just be a funny-coloured hog?

Most important for me at that moment was assessing the differences between *hughi* and her potential cohabitees. Looking at specimens like this can make it all feel too easy. They were clearly different – *auritus* has longer ears, *dauricus* was blonder and *hughi* had those distinctive dark-tipped spines. But would life in the field be so kind to us? After all, at least one of these hogs before me was used as a type specimen. There might be, as some authors suggest, quite considerable overlap between the species. In fact, some have gone so far as to suggest that there are far fewer than the twenty species mentioned by Nigel Reeve.

Still, my spirits were up. It was time to book a flight to China, meet Professor Wang Song and go find *hughi*. It is rare to find an academic so enthusiastic with an amateur enquiry and I was excited that I had not only his support but also his offer of travelling with me on a mission.

However, he had vanished. No replies came to my emails. So I waited a week and dropped him another line. Nothing. Waited a week and sent another email. Nothing. There were not quite beads of sweat forming, but there was a little knot of anxiety. He had made it clear he was going to be available for some of the month of June. Could I just accept that he would be free? Should I jump on a plane and hope that he would be around?

I waited another couple of weeks, sending regular emails. Fang Fang, a good friend of mine, is from China, so I persuaded her to phone the Institute of Zoology to see where the good professor was. No one knew.

I emailed more. I even phoned – hopelessly, because I speak no Mandarin, apart from hello, kiss and, obviously, hedgehog. *Ni hao, chin chin* and *ci wei*.

But nothing. I began to wonder about heading to China to look for Wang Song.

A search for him would require a guide, so I started to hunt for a guide to help me find Wang Song, who would help me find my hedgehog. I said it was not going to be simple.

A few false starts and then Roz Kidman Cox, former editor of the BBC *Wildlife Magazine* and the person who is perhaps most responsible for me doing what I am doing now (you can send letters of complaint to her in Bristol), told me about a fixer who had been working for the BBC in Beijing on a natural history series, setting up the filming of the weasels who have made their home in the centre of Beijing among the hutongs, the old back streets. An email to Poppy Toland was replied to immediately, with the added good fortune that she was in London, visiting family. No need to find a guide to find her at least.

She agreed to work with me. Not as prestigious as the BBC, but I think she was won over by the charm – of the hedgehog.

So, many months after I had originally planned to go, everything was in place. Ticket booked and visa queued for (in the spirit of sharing top tips for travel in China, go early to queue for the visa and go early to pick it up).

The bureaucracy was intense. The Forestry Department needed to know what we were up to, copies of visas and passports were sent, a letter from the British Hedgehog Preservation Society identifying me as a responsible hedgehog fanatic was written. And still there were problems.

It turned out there are a number of military bases in the area most likely to yield a *hughi* and there is a degree of sensitivity about allowing strangers to wander around with cameras and binoculars.

Plan B – always good to have a Plan B. In one of the documents I had copied from the Natural History Museum, Poppy was able to read a reference to Taiyuan. Not only did this have the advantage of being closer to Beijing, only a ten-hour train journey away, but it was also mercifully free from military complications. She booked the train tickets and I was set.

Of course, it was still a long shot. We didn't have anyone on the ground who would be able to help. We didn't know where to start looking. We were planning on rolling up in the city and then wandering around at random, showing people pictures of hedgehogs and trying to get a lead.

So I suggested that we formulate a Plan C, just in case. After all, it is always good to have a Plan C. But Plan C made Plan B seem like a pretty reasonable approach. Google listed a company that promised a remarkable service:

> We are Chinese medicinal animal nursary ground. Mainly, we nursary centipede, scorpion. We supply a great deal of dead, viable, centipede, scorpion, leech, flour beetle, hedgehog. all the year round. We can also help you outlet.
> Chuzhou, Anhui, China.

If the worst came to the worst, we would track down the man behind this enterprise Mr Liu Daming.

And so I was off. I didn't go the carbon-offsetting route to assuage my guilt for flying. I decided to take a lead from good Catholics and, while not quite the equivalent of self-flagellation, the cramped seats at the back of the crowded plane acted as, I am sure, suitable and rather intense penance.

The agonizingly long hours gave me time to think what it would have been like if I had approached this differently. If, for example, there had been some sort of organization ... Actually, I could leave it there – but I really wondered about being part of a large, professional outfit, backed by an institute of renown. Yet here I was, heading off on the most amateur of quests – doing it out of love and without money. Though the one time I did join a semi-organized outfit and spent three months searching for an extinct leopard in Morocco, I lost so much weight my clothes no longer fitted. Perhaps I was better on my own.

The one redeeming feature of the journey was the chance to start reading a new book. I have never delved into *Moby-Dick* before, but felt some kinship with Ahab and his quest, though perhaps without so much rage. Most unexpected was the early reference to a hedgehog, making it all the more appropriate, even if it was only in the mispronunciation of Queequeg that Peleg calls him Hedgehog.

The long and painful journey ended at the Lama Temple Hostel, where the silent and windowless womb of a room let me sleep for twelve and a half hours – the longest uninter-rupted sleep I have had for many years. Poppy yanked me from my dreamless repose with some vigorous banging on the door – I had missed our meeting by over four hours and she was beginning to get worried.

Blearily I followed her to her favourite café and there we spread out maps like the explorers we nearly were, tried to work out the merits of Plans A–C and wondered if there might be a D, E and F in the offing. Then, leaping from the 1930s to the present day, Poppy pulled out her laptop and logged on via wi-fi. And there we were: Plan A blown out of the water by bureaucracy, Plan B with many unknowns and plan C down to Google.

The café owner joined us and talked about her hedgehog memories: 'My brother used to catch them and keep them in a cage,' she said. This was just outside Beijing, but probably twenty years ago. She thought that they ate mice. She grinned as she made a rolling motion, showing what the hedgehog did when it was frightened. 'He would feed them things with a strong flavour,' she continued, 'and then they would make a strange coughing noise.' OK, so maybe her brother was a sadist, feeding chillies to hedgehogs. And maybe the coughing noise was rather like the beginning of self-anointing, the strange behaviour seen in European hogs.

As I paid our bill I noticed a bottle of liquid that looked not unlike some sort of rose water, but had, among the beautiful characters, the English words 'Toilet Water'. I mentioned this to Poppy, who explained that all over China there has been a spate of companies getting their products translated into English in the run-up to the Olympic Games, but the quality of the translation is open to question.

It has picked up the name 'Chinglish' and has given rise to some delightful confusions: a cake stall with the sign 'It is gluttonous to come quickly'; plum candies have the strapline 'Hey, so delicious, let us try it fast'; and a toilet in Shanghai with the sign 'Do not thrown urine around'. Though I wonder whether there might not be a temptation on the part of translators just to amuse the tourists.

Back in the world of hedgehogs, it seemed logical, but then again jet lag was kicking in, to head to the one person who claimed to know where to find hedgehogs. Poppy had spoken to Plan C, Liu Daming, and found that he would be happy to meet us and show us his hedgehogs. I tried to imagine what he would make of our interest; did he think we wanted to use them ourselves? And what species of hedgehog did he deal with? The distribution map I had photocopied back in London suggested the most likely species was *hughi*, but given the small number of sightings there have ever been, I didn't want to bet on it.

We could do no more, so Poppy took me to one of the many restaurants nearby, and thus began a new love affair with food. It was all very different from the Chinese food in Oxford. My mouth was tingling from a rare combination of pain and pleasure by the time I retired to the hostel.

The next day we reconvened in a rather unexpected café, Waiting for Godot. Established by a local businessman with a fondness for Beckett, the walls were dark. I picked up a copy of the *China Daily*, an English-language paper, and was delighted with a story that must fill all air travellers with the utmost confidence. Needless to say, I will not be flying on Nepal Airlines.

6 September 2007

Airline sacrifices goats

Officials at Nepal's state-run airline have sacrificed two goats to appease Akash Bhairab, the Hindu sky god, following technical problems with one of its Boeing 757 aircraft, the carrier said yesterday.

Nepal Airlines, which has two Boeing aircraft, has had to suspend some services in recent weeks due to the problems. The goats were sacrificed in front of the troublesome aircraft on Sunday at Nepal's only international airport, in Kathmandu, in accordance with Hindu traditions, an official said. 'The snag in the plane has now been fixed and the aircraft has resumed its flights,' said Rajun K. C., a senior airline official, without explaining what the problem had been.

I ordered coffee and received something like a quadruple espresso. My jet-lag-induced lethargy began to lift. We plotted some more, then headed for the station. Plan C was in motion and we were off, our train heading south.

Everyone in our full compartment had brought a feast with them. We had green tea out of little flasks filled from a boiler at one end of each carriage. And while some of those around us tucked into chicken feet, we ate the largest and most delicious pot noodles, spicy cabbage flavour.

We started to chat with the others in the compartment. There was quite a gang coming and going, and it turned out that this was the annual holiday for the Beijing Meitong Printing Company, off to Nanjing, with the Beijing Cheerful Holiday Tourist Company organizing everything. They were a great bunch and thought that I was mad. But we talked and soon stories about hedgehogs began to emerge.

'The hedgehog is treated with respect in Beijing,' explained Zhang Bao Dong, via Poppy. 'I have heard old people talking about the hedgehog and the weasel as spirit animals.' The last time he saw a hedgehog was when he was fishing in the outer suburbs of Beijing. He had put his box of bait on the ground and along snuffled a little hog. His eyes twinkled with joy as he described how it rolled up into a ball when he moved.

Cai Mingyou joined the conversation. 'I heard a cough when I was out one night and thought it was a person following me,' he said. 'But when I looked I couldn't see anyone. I looked around and found there was a hedgehog.' He also repeated the story about hedgehogs being 'spirit animals'. And then he started talking about how he was sure I was a vegetarian. This digression caused confusion until the compartment descended into laughter as it transpired he was talking about hedgehogs. This set them all off and as they continued to drink *baijiu* (rice wine) I could pick out references to *ci wei*, followed by more giggles, before everyone began to retire to their bunks and the carriage slipped swiftly into sleep.

There was a quick change in Nanjing, shortly after dawn, and on to Chuzhou. This journey gave me more time to mull over a worry that had hatched during the night. I wanted to find Hugh's hedgehog, and ideally I would do that in the company of expert field ecologists. I wanted to see my hedgehog out in the wild, doing natural hedgehoggy things. But here I was, following the only lead I had, heading towards a very different sort of hedgehog expert: someone who employs people to hunt for them so that the hedgehogs can be killed and used to make lotions, potions and pills. I was worried about what I would be confronted with. Battery-farmed *hughi*s? Cages of hedgehogs being fed slugs and beetles on a conveyor belt? And if this was what I saw, what would I do? I couldn't very well rescue a shed full of hedgehogs.

I was on the verge of getting a little sentimental about this – but it felt so wrong that I might be about to have my first meeting with a hedgehog I had fantasized about for so long and find it stuck in a cage like an unfortunate chicken. Did I want to see *hughi* so much that I would be content to let one suffer?

Chuzhou does not have many Western visitors judging by the attention we received on arrival; people took photographs. We walked away from the station and at random stopped at the third hotel we came to, booked in and dumped our bags. There was a great weight on my shoulders that remained even after removing my rucksack.

We had to decide what to do, so headed for brunch in a café around the corner. Yang Yang Xiu was so helpful. While her staff giggled and hid every time I looked towards them, she told us about Feng Le market and, while we relished her noodles, she mentioned that sometimes hedgehogs were seen there for sale.

Midday is probably not the best time to visit a market: everyone has shopped for lunch and evening business is a way off. But we took a walk around and Poppy started to ask questions. We walked by mounds of vegetables, great buckets of chillies, dried fungi, pyramids of spices and boxes of eggs. Pretty ropey-looking eggs too. I asked Poppy about them. These were, she told me, thousand-year-old eggs. My eyes widened, but she deflated my amazement by pointing out that the duck eggs were rarely more than 100 days old and had been buried in a large pot, covered in ash, salt and tea to aid fermentation.

Apparently my bilious reaction to the thought of eating the blackened egg was just the same as that of many in China to a plate of delicious blue-veined cheese. There are some delicacies that do not travel so well.

Through the meat section: this would give a Health and Safety officer nightmares. Cages of chickens packed close together. Chickens in a heap with their legs tied together looking up at other chickens having their throats cut, being boiled and plucked. A still-life of limp, pale ducks' necks. Then we were pointed further on, to a separate building: the fish hall. Fish are kept fresh by being kept alive. Boxes of eels writhed, crayfish hunched and carp pouted. In the very last corner we were told that it is extremely rare for someone to have a hedgehog, but we should try at the far end of the market, where we had just come from. So we trudged back, narrowly avoiding a squabble between two people busy gutting fish and kicking a large, glassy-eyed head back and forth.

On our way through the meat hall I slipped on some carelessly dropped intestines, much to the amusement of the massed ranks of butchers. And then we were back on the roadside. There was a woman selling chickens and eggs. She explained that sometimes someone would pitch up next to her with a hedgehog, but only early in the morning. I showed her the photographs I had taken in the museum back in London. Could she identify the sort of hedgehog? No. Maybe a long-eared one, maybe not. So we had to return before seven the next morning and hope our luck might change.

But this had all been a distraction from what I knew we must do. Here was a chance of seeing *hughi* and I was looking for ways out of it. I just did not want to deal with the horrors of intensively farmed hogs that I was picturing. However, I was a man on a mission and so we flagged down another taxi.

I imagine that Zhai Xiao Ming is still eating out on this fare. She was clearly surprised to have two English passengers, more surprised that one spoke fluent Mandarin and not entirely sure why we were heading thirty minutes out of town, up into the hills to pick up a man from a meat-roasting factory. That is where Liu Daming had a new business and it left me wondering in what form I would be finding my hedgehog.

We pulled up in a village and a stout man smiling broadly walked over and got in with us. Liu Daming did not strike me as a hedgehog torturer, but then what would one of those look like? He seemed really kind and enthusiastic, if a little confused. We carried on west until he pointed us off the main road and up a dirt track. We pulled up beside a large pile of charcoal and a very small compound. It did not seem that Liu Daming had quite the enterprise the Internet had promised.

He showed us into a room and disappeared briefly, before returning, gingerly holding . . . By this stage my mouth was dry as adrenalin surged through my system. Could it be this simple? I had been in China for just sixty hours and I had found a hedgehog that had been recorded just twelve times in the last 100 years. If someone from China had called me asking to see a hedgehog, apart from taking them to a hedgehog rescue centre, I doubt I could have guaranteed them such a swift result.

I am skirting around this to avoid the climax. It was like Christmas, getting a present from someone who knows exactly what you want but manages to get it not quite right.

It was clear, from the first glance, that this was not *hughi*. As Liu Daming opened his hands I could see that the spines were generally dusty brown and there was none of that distinctive dark tip I was so hoping for. But I had to smile like it was the Christmas present I had really wanted; I didn't want to seem ungrateful. He handed me the hedgehog. There was such a sense of familiarity. I had been expecting it to feel rather alien, but she – I checked, and showed Liu Daming how to tell – felt very like a hedgehog. Which, of course, she was. But you understand what I mean – sometimes familiarity can be a bit of a shock in alien surroundings.

She looked dehydrated and underfed, her nose was very dry and there was a 'narrowness' to her that looked unhealthy; but she was still perky enough and weighed in at 550 grams (important not to leave home without a spring balance, you never know when you might need one). And then it was time to take some photographs. I had, for as long as I was aware of Hugh's hedgehog, longed for a photograph of me and *hughi*. However poorly framed and exposed, I did not care, I wanted that photograph. Now I was going to have to be content with what appeared to be a Daurian hedgehog, *Hemiechinus dauricus*, as my partner. But first I got some pictures with Liu Daming and then I scrabbled around in the dirt, getting nose-to-nose with this little beast; nose-to-nose and nose to lens. She was really rather sweet. Not massively dissimilar to hedgehogs I have seen in the UK. She bristled like she should and slowly relaxed. Perhaps she had a more pronounced parting on her forehead? Her spines were different too. UK hogs tend to have a fairly similar sort of spine covering most of their back, but hers had a sprinkling of all cream ones. Her skirt of fur was pale as well, and this spread to her face, making her beady eyes

 stand out all the more clearly.

Poppy took over the role as photographer and this gave me a chance to pick up Dora, as she became known, for a closer look. Yes, there was a general

hedgehoggy smell, very mild, but definitely similar to ours in the UK. I looked into her eyes and felt a slight shift in my motivation. I had done, to a certain extent, what I had come to China to do – get a photograph of me with a hedgehog. And I know it was not the right hedgehog, but I was not even expecting to manage this, so I was thrilled. But I wanted more – and I was not even thinking about *hughi* now, but this individual. Throughout my work with hedgehogs I have shied away from 'individuals' – well, apart from the ones I named in Devon . . . OK, this is not entirely consistent, but I like to think I have shied away from sentimentality. So why was I now thinking of taking drastic action?

But what would Poppy think? She would undoubtedly dismiss me as a bit of a lightweight, getting soppy about a hedgehog. I handed Dora back to Liu Daming. Poppy came over and told me that while I was photographing her, he had turned to the taxi driver and said, 'He came all this way just to photograph a hedgehog? Next time he should just call me and I'll email him a picture.' Hardly the cutting edge of mammal research that first brought *hughi* to the attention of Oldfield Thomas. I got her to check and yes, this was the only hedgehog he had and he really did not get that many and he didn't breed them and, well, he really was not the enterprise the Internet suggested. What of the other animals? He beamed again and led me through to a dark and dirty room. He lifted a plastic lid on a box of muck and a few things scuttled. He reached in and showed, with great pride – in fact, with more excitement than when he revealed the hedgehog – a centipede with a bright red head. About 5 centimetres long, it sat on his palm as he continued beaming.

We went back out into the bright daylight and I was just wondering how I was going to break it to Poppy that maybe we should just buy Dora and then release her somewhere away from here, when she said quietly, 'We can't just leave her here. We must buy her and release her somewhere away from here.'

So it didn't have to be me being soft – it was all her fault. She asked how much. Liu Daming replied 100 yuan (about £7), though I am fairly sure he had mentioned something about twenty yuan when asked earlier. I pulled the note out of my pocket and he went to get Dora. He came back with a large polystyrene box, all bound up with twine.

We started to say goodbye, when it became clear that he was getting into the taxi with us for a lift back to the village where we met him. So we were not going to be releasing Dora quite yet, then. I wonder what he thought we were going to do with the hedgehog. Take it back to the UK? Barbecue it in our hotel room? I never did find out.

We let him out and said our farewells. Any time we were back this way we should drop by and say hi, he said. Then off he went to his meat-roasting business.

And what was the taxi driver thinking? A couple of kilometres out of the village we asked her to stop and I jumped out with the box, cut the twine and walked 100 metres or so away from the road. The area seemed uncultivated, there were no dwellings in sight and there was plenty of leaf litter, suggesting that there would be shelter and food to hand. I picked her up and placed her gently on the ground. That was the first time

I had ever 'owned' a wild animal and it was very brief. Just fifteen minutes. But it was great to see her relax, stick out her snout and begin to move. I left her to her new life. Maybe she would be picked up again tonight and end up in Liu Daming's dark room of beasts. Maybe she would be OK. Who knows? All I did was all I could do.

I suddenly felt very tired as I walked back to the taxi. It was time to go and lie down. We travelled back in silence, apart from Zhai Xiao Ming's horn, beeping everything out of her way.

Our next journey was to Hangzhou. This is where Poppy thought Father Hugh had been based when he found 'my' hedgehog, so it was possible that the city's natural history museum might hold a key bit of evidence. She explained that, over the years, the 'English' – or Pinyin – version of many names had changed and Hankow had become Hangzhou.

But before we could do that there was one more visit to be made. Early the next morning we made our way back to the Feng Le market. We had spent a long time discussing what we should do if we found hedgehog for sale. It is a very tricky area of debate. Having saved Dora, we were feeling filled with indignation at the treatment of hedgehogs and talked about buying the ones we found and heading out to the hills in the hope of releasing them far enough from human interference, all before catching a train at 8.20 a.m. But I was troubled by this: while it felt a good thing to do, there was a problem. If we turned up and started buying all the hedgehogs we saw, we would be seriously distorting the market. People would see that hedgehogs sold well (and over the odds if they were going to us) and try all the more to catch them. Therefore, reluctantly, we decided that we would have to just interview anyone we found with hogs, take photographs and then go. Leaving the hedgehogs to a pretty grim future.

We got a taxi to the market at 6.30. Poppy waited where we had been told the hedgehogs would be, if there were any, and I walked through the rest of the market, taking photos and searching for spiky beasts. I must have been doing something wrong when I said '*ci wei*'. Even when I tried so very hard to follow the instructions – first vowel is fourth tone, that is, descending, and the beginning has a subtle 't' before the sibilant opening – I still got nothing but blank looks. Back down to the boxes of eels, nothing, not one spine to be seen. So I weaved my way back to Poppy, through puddles of blood and piles of entrails.

She had also drawn a blank. The person who occasionally came with hedgehogs was not there and in fact had not been seen for quite some time. I felt simultaneous waves of relief and disappointment.

But I had missed something quite out of the ordinary. A man had arrived at the front of the market, squatted down, unwrapped a bundle and pulled out a stone. A fairly ordinary stone, about 30 centimetres across, that had one distinguishing feature, a pale impression of a cow. Poppy had a look. It seemed like a natural blemish. But who would buy a stone? She watched and listened, and within five minutes he had sold it for seventy yuan.

Hangzhou's museum of natural history deserves a special place in all guidebooks to the region. You must visit; there are sights within that will confound you and there are sights that will truly shock you. Oh, and there is a hedgehog. In fact, there is more than one; there is a mother with four babies.

In the corner of a case they were there among some unlikely companions: a pangolin, a tapir, a kangaroo and a rabbit. No more information than the Chinese symbols for '*ci wei*' made this rather frustrating. Which species was it? Where was it from? By pressing my nose against the glass, I could make out another piece of paper tucked under the hog's rump. Perhaps this might hold some answers.

Wu Yan was on duty and she was so helpful, eventually tracking down a professor who had the authority to enter the case, though we were not allowed in. He lifted the label and held it up to the window for us to read. Surprisingly the label said '*Erinaceus europaeus*', the European hedgehog, as found pottering around my garden in Oxford. It was hard to tell through the glass, as the beast looked very old and dusty, but it could have been. So why did the label say the specimen was found in China? It continued: 'Active in hedges, eats insects, small birds, birds eggs, frog skin, snakes, wild fruit, fungi, eats pests. Stomach and skin can be medically used.' Now, I had heard about this from Liu Daming, but it was interesting to see it referred to in the museum. Not that anyone there could enlighten us as to how hedgehogs are used.

Later we did track down some information, which Poppy translated: 'It [the hedgehog] is used to cure "the five haemorrhoids". For persistent diarrhoea the hedgehog skin should be roasted . . . and then ground into a fine powder. For seminal emission hedgehog skin should be roasted and add flowery dragon bone, ground together into a fine powder. Use honey to roll them into round pills – as big as small beans.' There was also a recipe for curing a bad stomach, though you might think that would be the result of the remedy.

When I got back to the UK and asked around the Traditional Chinese Medicine community I was met with an absolute and rather defensive reaction. In the UK there are no animal parts used, legitimately at least, in TCM, and when a teacher from the register of Chinese Herbal Medicine, Tony Booker, scoured the archives, he could find no references to hedgehogs. Worms and turtles, yes, but not hedgehogs.

I also found out that Hankow had not changed its name and is in fact still very happily existing not a million miles from where we had been. So next time Poppy comes back to London she is going to buy me as lovely a meal as Chinatown has to offer in compensation.

Back in Beijing, I met some human Hedgehogs. The two members of Hedgehog, Shi Lu and Zi Jian, aka Atom and ZO, were a disgrace to the stereotype of noisy pop stars. You could not imagine a more delightful and polite couple of people to share lunch with. Atom was around 1.50 metres tall, delicate and powerful. She was unlike any other rock drummer I had met. Her collaborator, ZO, was a tall and nervously thin guitarist.

Their career to date has seen them needing to retain their day jobs. But their second album, *Noise Hit World*, launched towards the end of 2007, was with a leading Indy label, so perhaps their brand of NoisePoP will allow them to fulfil their dreams of going full-time. Even since I met them, their presence has expanded on the web, where you can get to hear the NoisePoP as loud as you wish. Their CD is an unlikely regular on my hi-fi and I am beginning to find it strangely endearing.

Why did they call themselves Hedgehog? There is disagreement about the name. Atom is concerned: 'A hedgehog is a spiritual animal, a special animal that is treated with respect, so it feels a little wrong, maybe presumptuous, to call ourselves that.'

But ZO was undeterred and in fact saw a reflection of himself in the hedgehog. 'It is a very individual animal,' he explained. 'And if it doesn't want to interact with the world, it retreats into its protective coat. But he can be very friendly if he wants. Sometimes I just don't want to talk to people and I can be just like that. I retreat and get rather prickly. But the main reason why I like the hedgehog is that this is a small animal that really knows how to look after itself.'

'But we must not ignore the fact that it is a spiritual animal,' Atom insisted. 'Like the fox and the weasel, you must not hurt it unnecessarily. My uncle told me that if he was outside and a fox suddenly appeared and looked at him, he would know that he was going to receive bad luck. But I don't think that the hedgehog is quite such an omen.'

Hedgehogs remain portentous in China, just like they were in Britain before the arrival of Mrs Tiggy-Winkle. I wonder if a Chinese Beatrix Potter is ready to help shift opinions.

A bit of digging when I got home revealed an

article in a 1948 edition of the journal *Folklore*: 'On the Cult of the Four Sacred Animals in the Neighbourhood of Peking'. Atom was absolutely right that there is a deep attachment to hedgehogs in this part of China. Foxes, weasels and snakes are the other be-culted beasts. The *pai-men* (the hedgehog family) is treated with great reverence and linked with the God of Wealth. And the review of beliefs throws new light on the age-old question of why there are so many hedgehogs squashed on the road. Hedgehogs are attempting to facilitate their spiritual journey to nirvana. 'When a certain stage on the way to perfection is reached, the hedgehog will be compelled by its own soul-power (*ling-hsing*) to lay itself down on the road in the tracks of vehicles out of longing for being crushed by the wheels.'

So how does such a reverence for the animal sit with a desire to slice it up for medicine? Atom had a thought on this: 'Chinese medicine has a long history. Maybe the superstitions of people without much education have infected the practice so that they would use the hedgehog, disregarding the tradition of respect.'

Poppy explained to them what we had been doing and how we had found a hedgehog for sale in Anhui Province. ZO asked what the hedgehog was being sold for and we explained that it was probably food or medicine. He thought for moment and concluded, 'Well, we won't be playing in Anhui then.'

As Hedgehog zoomed off to their other lives as mere mortals, it dawned on me that time was accelerating. In thirty-six hours I would be on a plane home. Despite this being such a short trip I really felt that I had achieved quite a lot. I had found a hedgehog, rescued a hedgehog, had lunch with two Hedgehogs and found a stuffed family in a museum.

On my last full day we headed to Beijing Zoo. As we scoured the place I noticed a small office: Wild China. I had been in touch with them when trying to find a guide earlier in the year and wondered whether Lihong Shi might be around. She has established a wonderful enterprise. Not only does she run a film company specializing in the wildlife of China, but she has also set up a project with Zhi Nong Xi, an internationally respected and award-winning wildlife photographer, to teach conservation workers how to take photographs.

They were in – apparently a rare thing, as they are so busy. This spontaneous meeting was amazingly timed. Zhi Nong Xi had just received a photograph from one of his students. Well, a very mature student, in that Mr Ai Huaisen is the senior warden at the Gaoligonghsan Nature Reserve in Yunnan Province. It was of a hedgehog and this was the perfect chance to see if I could identify which species.

As the image appeared on the screen I gave an involuntary gasp. This was something so very different from anything I had seen in China so far. In fact, I had never seen a photograph like it; the dark-tipped spines were so distinctive. This could be nothing other than *Hemiechinus hughi*. Hugh's hedgehog had been photographed. I was so excited that I forgot I had wanted the honour of capturing this image. It meant that the distribution map I had been using was off by over 1,600 kilometres in terms of the southern extent of *hughi*'s range. I was due to leave the country in a little over thirty hours and the hedgehog had been found in a reserve that was four hours' drive away from a railway station that was forty-six hours away from where I was. So that was that. Hugh's hedgehog was still extant, but there was no way I could get to it before my flight. I felt a wave of calm resignation. I had got pretty far down the road to *hughi* and now I had a much better idea of where to start should I come to China again.

We chatted some more and I found out useful information about Professor Wang Song as well. He was not ignoring me; he had retired and was spending his time as far from his desk as possible, travelling to nature reserves all over the country, enjoying himself, but as busy as he ever was while officially employed. Reminds me rather of my mentor, Pat Morris, now retired and busier than ever.

We parted fondly. I had really warmed to the team of Wild China. They even put in a call to track down a keeper to tell us more about the zoo's hedgehogs. Yang Yi was enthusiastic, but not a specialist. His world revolved around the red pandas, very distant relations to the rather overexposed monochrome variety. He took us to a dark concrete building and showed us an enclosure. The argumentative giant flying squirrel prevented us entering to get a closer look at the two hedgehogs hunkered down in the corner. The sign said '*Erinaceus europaeus*', but they were clearly different from 'our' hog. I asked Yang Yi where they had come from: they had been found in the grounds of the zoo. They are seen in May and June, early in the mornings or late at night, snuffling in the undergrowth surrounded by the staggering development of this enormous city.

I have written to the zoo explaining that their label is wrong and have also made a few suggestions as to how to improve the welfare of these poor captives. I hope that they have taken note, as it is a shame to see animals treated with such scant regard for their welfare in the twenty-first century.

And now I was done I suddenly realized how tired I was. I returned to the hostel, packed, and headed off for a last supper with Poppy. The food, oh, the food was stunning: young bamboo, egg and jasmine flowers, wood ear fungus and palm hearts, red cabbage and spring onions, mint salad, kohlrabi and buckwheat noodles, all washed down with Yanjing beer. The flavours and textures combined to create one of the most extraordinarily amazing meals I have ever experienced. It was a fitting farewell to Poppy and the city.

As I collapsed into the uncomfortable plane seat I was hit by a wave of disappointment. I had failed. I had known that this was a lunatic challenge, but I had hoped. Still, at least I had met and held a Chinese hedgehog. Dear Dora, I hope she managed to survive the hostilities of her home. Strange that was the very first time I had ever 'owned' a wild animal. Just such a shame that she was not *hughi*. And then, in spite of the hum of the plane and the numbing tiredness, I had a moment of inspiration.

These are rare events and it generated a crackling energy through my body that threatened to break the seat belt with the tension. When I went to meet Liu Daming and bought

Dora, I had her in my possession for a good fifteen minutes. And for that short time, there was no doubting the fact that she was Hugh's hedgehog. I spent much of the journey grinning to myself, unable to share the news, but desperate to tell everyone.

I had done it; sort of. I had found Hugh's hedgehog.

PART THREE

Save the Hedgehog — Save the World

CHAPTER
SEVEN

*How We Can
Look After
Hedgehogs*

Can you imagine a world without hedgehogs? Would you notice the gaping void in your life if you never again heard the snuffling in your undergrowth? Perhaps it wouldn't hit you immediately, but I am sure that an absence of hedgehogs would have a far more profound effect on us than the disappearance of pandas, tigers or whales.

When, in 2007, the Environment Agency sought a new icon for its work in England and Wales it asked people to vote for the species or habitat that most represented their view of the natural world. Oak trees and bluebell woods, otters and robins all got nominated. But then someone added the hedgehog – and it became the runaway winner, defeating more obviously charismatic contenders. It is clear that hedgehogs are special to very many people. If they disappeared from this island, if such an everyday animal could be discarded, what would that mean for us? Would we see their demise as an alarm bell for our own precarious position?

A hedgehog-free Britain isn't going to happen any time soon, but there are grounds for concern. Hedgehogs are pretty robust critters. In some form or other they have been around since the appearance of mammals, with early versions nipping at the heels of the departing dinosaurs. They have survived ice ages, outlasted mammoths and sabre-toothed tigers and even managed to form a symbiotic relationship with those arch-predators, humans. But the headlines are clear: hedgehogs are under threat.

The concern began, once again, because of Pat Morris. Starting in 1987, he undertook roadkill surveys. This has grown into the 'Mammals on Roads' project run by the Mammals Trust, where volunteers count corpses they see on specific journeys.

This begs an interesting question. If lots of hedgehogs are seen on the road, does that mean there are few hedgehogs alive in the surrounding area as most have been killed, or that there are lots as there are so many available for the motorcar? Well, a single data point does not tell you much. But repeating the survey builds a picture of fluctuations in numbers – as long as hedgehogs do not suddenly learn to avoid cars, that is. It seems that the number of corpses correlates well with the number of hedgehogs: the more hedgehogs in an area, the more likely that squashed ones will be seen.

Why do there seem to be so many hedgehogs killed? Are they killed more frequently than other species? Is it because they roll up when threatened rather than run away? I can actually answer some of these questions. The reason why we see so many hedgehogs is partly because of their spines. They last a lot longer as a reminder of the collision. The remnants of a rabbit are going to be pilfered away by a crow or gull, but the little Frisbee of prickles remains to haunt other travellers.

There is a lovely story I have seen in three places so far, though in each case the details are slightly different and it seems to be taking on the qualities of an urban myth. A man, in one instance a carpetfitter from Doncaster, of large and rather scary proportions, hid a deep love for wildlife, and hedgehogs in particular, behind a maze of tattoos. There was a particular patch of road where he noticed hedgehogs getting squashed on a regular basis. So much so that he believed there must be some deliberate targeting going on. He formulated a plan; the hedgehog's revenge. He collected a recently deceased individual, took it home and carefully gutted it on the kitchen table. He then put a brick inside the skin and returned it to the road, where he placed it and waited for the inevitable collision.

I read a version of this in one of the Bogor cartoons from New Zealand's *Listener* magazine, I read it in a small English regional newspaper and I read it in the *Sunday Times*. In this last outing, the story began, 'This story must be true as I heard it on Radio 4.' But what this columnist had not noticed was that it was a humorous programme called '*Foot Off the Pedal*' and it was me who was spinning wild tales.

Would hedgehogs fare any better if their defensive strategy evolved into something more active? This is a moot point. Given the speed at which hedgehogs move, perhaps staying still is not such a bad option. Obviously staying still in the path of a wheel is bad, but given that more of the car is not wheel, the chance is that the hedgehog would not be in the line of the tyre.

But if they move, there is the risk that they move from safety into the path of the wheel.

People notice hedgehogs, and they notice the absence of hedgehogs too. I have given hundreds of talks about hedgehogs and one of the most repeated comments is that 'there just don't seem to be as many hedgehogs as there used to be'. Now, most of my audiences tend to be of retirement age, often Women's Institute (I have started to demand part-payment in cake), and I did wonder whether this was a romantic memory, like people being politer and food being tastier back in the old days.

But there was a consistency with the anecdotes that began to give them credibility. Everywhere the story seemed to be the same. While writing this book, when people have asked what I am doing they nearly always tell stories of seeing fewer hedgehogs. I have not met a single person who has told me that they are seeing more hedgehogs now than in the past.

The data from Pat and the Mammals Trust began to add some very disturbing meat to the bones of the story. Hedgehog numbers appeared to be in the sort of free-fall that, if found in birds, would result in questions being asked in Parliament. But a lowly mammal, however popular, has to struggle in the face of the avian conspiracy.

The Mammals on Roads survey revealed that between 2001 and 2005 there was a national decline in hedgehogs of 20 per cent. For some regions, including East Anglia, over a slightly longer period, the decline reached 50 per cent. This caused the British Hedgehog Preservation Society and the People's Trust for Endangered Species to take notice. The figures were serious and what was more worrying was that we did not know the cause. To try to find out we raised money to fund a PhD student to look at the many factors affecting hedgehog survival. During this time we all got involved in one project, HogWatch. This was the first survey of its kind and it relied upon the hedgehog's most important characteristic – its appeal. The aim of HogWatch was to get enough data to produce a map of where hedgehogs had been seen in the UK and, more importantly, where they had not. And to do this we needed people, lots of people, to tell us what they knew.

There is a view that science is done by other people, in lab coats. But there are times when nothing can compete with the amateur. While we managed to get many responses via the membership of our organizations, it was the media that really helped propel the story into the public arena. I did countless radio and television interviews, newspapers picked up the story and we were inundated with gorgeous information. Thanks to the 20,000 people who responded, we could start to produce a nationwide map in 2007.

What a story this map told. There was a clear east–west split in areas where hedgehogs were most likely to be seen. Now, I had always felt, based on nothing other than prejudice, that the west was the natural home of the hedgehog. The moister land, the smaller fields and the cows all struck me as perfect. But the dominant side for hedgehogs is the east.

While this was a surprise, it was also worrying, as it is the east of the country where the decline in hedgehog numbers has been the greatest. Had a decline already occurred in the west?

What were the factors that made the apparently suitable land so hostile to the hogs? We are beginning to understand more about what is happening, but these questions are all part of the ongoing survey.

First, a word about badgers. At the BHPS we regularly receive letters from farmers asking us to join them in taking up arms against the evil Brock. As badgers eat hedgehogs they assume that we will want to join with them in wiping the fiends off the face of earth. And our results from HogWatch do reveal an apparent correlation between the increase in badgers and the decrease in hedgehogs. Perhaps we should be calling for the end of the badger . . . or perhaps we should be looking a little more closely at what is going on.

Farmers want to rid the countryside of badgers because badgers are blamed for transmitting bovine TB to cattle. But there is another reason why the farming community wants to see the back of the badger. In the press this is phrased as an effort to increase the breeding success of ground-nesting birds, the eggs of which are stolen by greedy badgers.

But how altruistic is this stance? Not as much as it might at first appear. The birds that the farming union is most keen to preserve are not the skylark or the lapwing, but the game birds, such as pheasant and partridge, the eggs of which will occasionally fall into the mouths of passing badgers. And I find it hard to get exercised about game birds that thrive at the whim of the hunting industry.

Are badgers responsible for the vanishing hogs? This is tricky. And I am not entirely impartial, having witnessed my Little Willy being devoured by a ravening beast from hell.

We know that, locally, badgers can have quite an impact. Not just from what I observed, but also from researchers at Oxford University. So clear were the results from a study they did on releasing hedgehogs into the badger-rich environment around Wytham Woods in Oxfordshire, published in 1992, that I heard more than one biologist refer to their efforts as badger-feeding experiments. Though another scientist at the university has told me that the story of Wytham's hedgehogs is more complicated than just badgers. The locals tell of Gypsies, not badgers, eradicating hedgehogs from the wood.

Wytham Woods is the most studied woodland in the country. I have spent many happy, sleepless nights surveying small mammals around the margins. Badgers and deer frequent the glades, and the bluebells – each year I try to get up to the woods to walk through the haze of blue.

So do badgers control hedgehogs? And if so, perhaps some should be released on to the Uists to help SNH with their tricky problem (that way lies madness – the madness that resulted in the cane toad exterminating all in its path in Australia after it was deliberately released in 1935 to control the cane beetle).

At first glance it would seem that the farmers have got a point. Under the Protection of Badgers Act (1992), it is illegal to interfere with badgers and their setts, overturning generations of persecution – both in the form of (perceived) vermin control and for the 'sport' of badger baiting. Since then badger numbers appear to have increased.

Has that corresponded with a decline in hedgehogs? We do not know. There seem to be fewer hedgehogs where there are more badgers. But this does not necessarily mean there is what is known as a causal relationship. It is possible that changes in the landscape and farming practice are creating a situation where the hedgehog and the badger are forced together in smaller pockets of suitable habitat.

Frustratingly there seems to be evidence of a solution that would meet everybody's needs. Research has shown that smaller fields with richer hedges contain cattle that suffer less from TB, despite the presence of badgers. These are also habitats that would benefit hedgehogs. But the way things are going, it doesn't seem likely that numbers of smaller fields will ever increase.

One of the answers we have is that there is a clear correlation between increased field size and reduced hedgehog numbers. This is all part of 'habitat fragmentation'. Hedgehog heaven involves hedges. Obvious really. Now hedges are no longer allowed to be ripped up for fun, or grant payments, as they once were. They can only be destroyed through the planning system, which should not fill any hedge lover with confidence. And there is another problem out there – the diggers might have stopped grubbing out hundreds of years of ecological heritage in the quest for a fraction more farmland, but the

skilled workers who knew how to manage a hedge have been grubbed out too. One of the sorriest sights from a train window, as I barrel along through the countryside, is the vision of a line of trees separated by a few bits of scrub and held together by wire fencing. This is a dead hedge. Hedges die if they don't get laid (I am sure there is a joke in there somewhere).

The loss of hedges is important. Hedgehogs spend 60 per cent of their time within 5 metres of a hedge or woodland edge and 80 per cent of hedgehog nests are found within them. Hedges are the highways and byways of the countryside, used by many species, but particularly by hedgehogs – they hog the hedges – and even more particularly by nursing mothers, whose young will be hidden in a hedge, and who will not want to travel far from the safety the hedge promises.

Their demise reduces the hedgehog's ability to traverse the land. This prevents replenishment of hedgehog populations that get wiped out by badgers, disease or cars. Birds, bats and insects transcend these barriers, but hedgehogs are blocked. It is a shame that many of the measures of the value of bio-diversity are based on birds, bats and insects. If mammals such as the hedgehog were the measure of a land's fitness, perhaps more would be done to prevent its degradation.

Another problem faced by rural hedgehogs is 'improved pasture'. Superficially this is the sort of habitat that you might imagine any self-respecting hedgehog would adore: lush grass suggestive of an invertebrate feast just waiting to be snaffled up by an inquisitive snout. But this verdant landscape is not quite what it seems.

The issue is in the 'improved' bit. Traditional pasture is maintained with few external inputs. Fertilizer comes from the cows that crop the rich grass and the many intermingled herbs add great diversity to the ecosystem. How could this be improved? Well, it all depends on what you are measuring. If it is a very basic measure of amount of milk per hectare, then the use of agrochemicals and single grass varieties will help. If the measure is of a diverse and sustainable ecosystem, then it will not.

It seems likely that the problem hedgehogs face in an 'improved' habitat is that there is less diversity, so fewer bugs to eat. Strange that the landscape farmers are claiming to be defending for us is less attractive to wildlife than the amenity grasslands provided by local councils. As it is to suburbia that the hedgehogs appear to have flocked, for now at least.

The fate of the UK's hedgehogs is not clear, but it seems that we have good reason to worry. It is a testament to the power of Beatrix Potter, perhaps, that we do worry, as hedgehogs have not always been the loved creatures they are now.

Not everyone loves Mrs T

Reading this book, you might have got the impression that our relationship with hedgehogs is a real-life rom-com of mismatched cuteness, tragedy, misunderstanding, slapstick and underlying love. It has not always been thus.

Over the centuries there has been a systematic assault on our dearly beloved friend. The conservationist and author Roger Lovegrove has researched this assault, in the years following his retirement from the RSPB. He took himself into the dark corners of early bureaucracy, spending an age rummaging through 450 years' worth of parish records that reported the extermination of 'vermin'. It was all recorded, as payment was made on presentation of proof of extermination. His results were published in 2007 in *Silent Fields: The Long Decline of a Nation's Wildlife*, which for the first time revealed the remarkable scale of the slaughter.

Vermin – we all know what vermin are, things like rats. But hedgehogs? How did they get to be verminous? How could our cute, adorable Mrs Tiggy-Winkle warrant a bounty? Because that is what happened. This was not just a random assault on animals over a few centuries, but a concerted effort, rewarded by payment.

The official start of the campaign began with Queen Elizabeth I passing the Vermin Act in 1566. There were some staggering 'bags'. The Cheshire parish of Bunbury records that 8,585 hedgehogs were killed in thirty-five years in the late seventeenth century.

Why the hostility? The accepted reasons were that hedgehogs were egg thieves and that they stole milk from cows. The egg-eating has undoubtedly got an element of truth in it, but suckling cows? I fear that this must be in the same category as the fruit-carrying myth. But likewise, repetition has given it credibility. There are many stories in the archives of folklore that tell of people who have definitely seen it happening with their own two eyes.

The problems are obvious: a hedgehog's mouth is too small and its teeth too sharp. There is, however, a logical explanation for the source of the story. Early morning, cows lying around, chewing the cud and gossiping. Sometimes there will be a little seepage from the teats. Now, we know that hedgehogs like milk, so a little inquisitive snuffling may well lead a hungry hog to a few drips, which would be consumed with delight, I am sure. But then along comes the herdsman or milkmaid or whoever did that sort of early-morning job and what do they see? A hedgehog with milky chops and a cow with a little puddle of spilt juice. What would you think? And then if the yields were down, there was the explanation.

When things go wrong, as they did a lot for sixteenth-century rural communities of England, thanks to disease, poor weather and worse harvests, there is a need to find a 'scapehog'. People couldn't beat up the weather, so they turned to wildlife. It may well have been a simple case of ignorance about hedgehogs – with people really believing that they were having an impact on the food supplies – but I also wonder whether this was all part of a tacit social security system for some of the most vulnerable in the community. Could it be that the authorities were well aware that hedgehogs were not vermin, but that by labelling a very easily caught animal as such, this was a way of giving money to the needy for performing a socially useless function in the guise of a socially useful function?

The fact that parishes were paying twice as much for a hedgehog as they were for a stoat or weasel suggests that this was not a scale based on potential damage to productivity.

There was the added advantage that, as only

the head needed to be presented, the rest of the body could be eaten, so killing hedgehogs was definitely a win-win situation (though not for the hedgehog).

Lovegrove extrapolates from the data he was able to collect to provide an idea of the national scale of the destruction levelled on the innocent urchins. He estimates that in the ten counties he has most data for around half a million hedgehogs were killed between 1660 and 1800.

Very roughly, that would correspond to a nationwide cull of 2 million over 140 years – so about 14,000 per year. That sounds awful. But consider the present day. While there may be a few gamekeepers and conservationists flying in the face of mainstream opinion by actively killing hedgehogs, Pat Morris has estimated 15,000 are killed each year on the roads. So I do not think we can judge our ancestors too harshly.

Given this slaughter, what can we do to help?

A Hedgehog-friendly Garden

I am always asked how to improve the lot of the hedgehog – usually straight after being asked about sex and fleas. I love the question, as it gives me a chance to go on about how we can all make a difference – how even the smallest patch of garden can be improved for wildlife and how a great interconnectedness between all things is revealed by this. And sometimes I just use the short answer: do less gardening. The tidier the garden, the more likely it is that slugs will feast inappropriately. Removing

those enticing heaps of decaying leaves will leave your strawberries as fair game. Interfere less and nature's order will take
care of both your hedgehogs and your strawberries.

If we want to actively improve our patch for hedgehogs, we
need to make it a little more like what a hedgehog would enjoy.
Remember the 'hedge' in the name. Think about the qualities a
good old hedge possesses and see how best to replicate them
in your garden.

Consider how wonderful hedgehogs are for the garden.
Known as the gardener's friend by many, the hedgehog is well
versed at getting rid of several of the most irritating invertebrates – those slugs and snails that can break a gardener's
heart. In fact, so good are they that I have met two people
who have discussed the idea of harnessing this passion and
offering it as a service. One was quite serious about trying to set
up a hedgehog farm from where he would supply hedgehogs
to gardens and allotments (the last I heard of him was that
he had been sectioned somewhere in Africa). The other idea
was more in jest, I think. Someone suggested establishing a
hedgehog SWAT team (Special Weapons and Tactics becoming
Spiny Weapons against Torment, or possibly, if they came
from Yorkshire, Spiny Weapons against t'molluscs). Colonies
of hedgehogs could be called in to deal with problem gardens
and allotments. A hedgehog-proof barrier would be erected
and the highly trained and incentivized (i.e. hungry) operatives
would be let loose on the verminous invertebrates. I sense more
reality TV on the horizon.

At the BHPS we have published a series of pamphlets that

outline the best ways we can increase the chances of hedgehogs coming to our gardens and how, when they are there, we can reduce their chances of coming to an untimely end. We know that hedgehogs help to control some of the most irritating of garden pests, so let us see what we can do to return the favour.

Bonfires – I love them. There is something quite primal (or is this just a man thing) about lighting and feeding a good fire on a Sunday afternoon. I have such distinct memories of my father coming in smelling of smoke, ruddy-cheeked and happy, for tea. But talk to any wildlife rescue centre and they will tell you horror stories of half-cooked hedgehogs being rescued. The easiest way to avoid barbecuing your spiny friend is to use a proper incinerator, or to move the pile prior to lighting, just to check that no one has taken up residence underneath.

Netting – I remember rescuing birds that had got caught in the netting over my parents' raspberry canes. This netting needs to be around 30 centimetres off the ground if it is to avoid horrible injury to hedgehogs. They have a tendency to get tangled and their reaction to an unexpected interruption to their travel will be to roll up, worsening the problem. The same goes for all netting – football, tennis – it can all catch and kill hedgehogs.

Ponds – Our pond is a little like the Bank of England, fortified to prevent our children, Mati and Pip, taking involuntary swimming lessons. The mesh across the top is fine enough to stop hedgehogs getting in, but large enough for frogs to escape. But not everyone has such a formidably protected puddle in their garden. Now, hedgehogs need to drink, so they will be attracted to the welcome water. And they can swim, so if they fall in, all is not lost. But they cannot swim forever. If the pond has smooth and steep sides, the poor beast will eventually drown. So provide an escape route, a gentle ramp, plastic-coated wire, plants to provide purchase. I met a man from Southampton who was so distressed to find a dead hedgehog floating in his pond that he completely redesigned his water feature to include, as he put it, 'a beach'.

Bear in mind unintentional ponds such as sandpits and buckets that can get filled with rain.

Drains – Keep drain holes covered. This stops both leaves and hedgehogs from causing blockages – remember, they don't flush well. If there are unavoidable voids, like garage inspection pits, then they need to be checked daily, or provided with an escape route.

Fences – These can present barriers to the free movement of hedgehogs through suburbia, so make sure that, if you want to encourage visitors, you leave space for them to come and go as they please. And think about what you protect the wood

with. I remember the welts I came out in after creosoting a fence. There are now plenty of gentler preservatives on the market. Hedgehogs will often have an exploratory lick of new additions to the olfactory menu, so make sure this is not their final experience.

Wild Patches – I would always encourage small portions of wilderness in a garden, partly to accommodate my laziness, but also because it is these patches that provide both food and shelter for hedgehogs. Piles of logs and stones can create a home for hedgehog food and, if big enough, a hedgehog. But remember, should you be tempted to rein in the florid excess, please take care if using a strimmer. These devices mutilate hedgehogs with horrifying efficiency. If you must go through long grass, cut first at 30 centimetres off the ground and then check for wildlife before cutting lower. You can supplement your mini-wilderness with some strategic planting of other wildlife-friendly flowers and herbs.

Compost – We had a wonderful compost heap that provided rich pickings for a wide range of wildlife until the rats got too presumptuous. Now we put only garden waste there. Compost heaps are great places for hedgehogs to nest and even to rear young. They are warm and filled with hedgehog food. So please take care if you want to turn your heap. Just sticking a fork into its heart could be disastrous.

Slug Pellets – The most common slug pellets contain metaldehyde, which is known to kill hedgehogs. There are alternative products, but see if you can find

a better solution. There is great satisfaction to be had from nightly expeditions with a sharp stone, slicing open slugs near your crop. You can make this more efficient by luring the slugs with something they like even more than lettuce. Sow some marigolds as a 'companion' plant to keep the slimy wretches occupied or leave grapefruit skins, another great attractant. I have had good success with beer traps (using very cheap beer in a yoghurt pot, buried so it is flush with the ground), but I stopped after I killed two newts and some rather interesting-looking beetles. And remember, slug pellets don't just kill the slugs that eat your pansies, they also kill the slugs that help generate a healthy soil by being detritivores, and they kill the slugs that form part of the hedgehog's diet. They are also dangerous to pets, birds and children.

Litter – Now, hopefully your garden is not covered in litter, but even small amounts can cause misery. The plastic rings around four-packs of drink are lethal. A young hedgehog getting caught in one will be unable to escape and will continue to grow until the plastic has eaten into its flesh. Other bits of plastic that can cause harm are things like yoghurt pots that may lure a hedgehog into deeper investigation, but then prevent escape as the spines prevent the hog from reversing out. There was a famous case of McDonald's, for one of the first times in its career, backing down in the face of protest. McFlurry desserts came in a pot with an opening large enough to allow an inquisitive hedgehog to get trapped. Pictures of hedgehogs killed in this way were sent to the BHPS, which then began a quiet yet persistent campaign, resulting in the redesign of the lids around the world.

Sheds – For some, people as well as hedgehogs, these are a place of refuge. Hedgehogs are not put off by human buildings and will use them to shelter. But if you have left your shed open for a few weeks and then decide to close it, what will come of a nest of hoglets trapped inside? Have a look around. And shift any poisons up a bit. Rescuers often get calls in June from people who have decided to dismantle a shed and found that a mother and her babies were sheltering beneath it. If you can, save such major works for October, when there are no babies and hibernation has yet to begin. And again, consider what you treat the wood with.

Dogs – Don't get me wrong, I love dogs (and I quite like cats, even though my neighbours think I am a tad vigorous in my defence of nesting birds), and one day I will live with a dog again. But dogs can kill hedgehogs – I am sure it was a dog that did for one of my radio-tracked hedgehogs in Scotland. So if you have a dog with a thing about hedgehogs, try warning hedgehogs in the garden before letting the hound out at night, maybe with an outside light. Or consider putting it on a lead.

Feeding – So much of what I have just written is a bit negative – don't do this, don't do that. But there are some very positive things you can do to increase the chances of hedgehogs

visiting your home (always bearing in mind the transcendental hedgehog and remembering that success is not guaranteed). There are three things a hedgehog needs to feel at home: food, water and shelter. Bread and milk used to be considered the staple hedgehog food and hedgehogs love them – but my daughter loves sweets and that does not mean they are good for her. Hedgehogs do not digest cow's milk very well, so they can end up with diarrhoea. And while they will eat bread, they are insectivores, meaning that they are designed for eating animals. Whatever Aristotle may have thought, hedgehogs are not vegetarianly inclined.

If you have a hedgehog-friendly garden, you will not need to provide water as there will be some around. But if the weather is dry, there is no harm in putting some out. The easiest food is just tinned pet food, though you can buy specially formulated hedgehog food – Spike's Dinner. You will need to leave the food under something low to stop cats and dogs getting at it. An upturned box, with a little doorway cut into it and a stone on top (to prevent the craftier cats and dogs getting at the contents), should be fine. And if you are lucky you will attract regular visitors. I have met people who end up being persecuted by 'their' hedgehogs – they turn up and if they find an empty dish, they start to clatter it noisily until they receive the attention to which they have become accustomed. But don't worry, studies have been done to show that they manage quite well without you.

Hedgehog Homes – While a hedgehog will probably be happy with a patch of wildness, you can supplement accommodation possibilities. Same idea as the food really, the best bet is to have a garden with natural food and natural shelter, but a little extra won't hurt.

The best place for a hedgehog home is in a quiet part of the garden, preferably against a bank, wall or fence. If you can face it so the entrance is to the south, this will allow the hedgehog to warm more quickly and reduce cold winds nipping a sleeping hog's toes. It is worth considering giving it a spring clean to prevent the build-up of parasites that might hide away in old bedding. The best time is early April, when residents will be out of hibernation and not yet at the baby stage. How do you know if it is occupied? A little bit of detective work. Put a light obstacle in the doorway and the next day if you find it is pushed in, someone is inside; if it is pushed out, they have left; and if it is still upright, the place is unoccupied. But be careful, just in case. A little bit of organic pyrethrum powder, suitable for caged birds, will take care of the unwanted bugs.

Sometimes hedgehogs will make use of the most unusual homes. I got a letter from a Mr Percy Ponting of Kent, who had been having a pleasant cup of tea with the vicar when they were interrupted by a strange noise. Further investigation revealed a hedgehog pulling the stuffing out of one of the sofa cushions. To reach the sofa the hedgehog would have had to climb steps and walk through three rooms. Mr Ponting had no idea how long it had been resident, but after carrying it into the garden the vicar pointed out that he was probably the first of his kind to exorcize a hedgehog.

Accidental Disturbance – That is by you of a hedgehog, not courting hedgehogs creating mischief in the bushes or nibbling your soft furnishings. If you uncover a hedgehog nest, do not panic. If there is an adult there, simply replace the nesting material and it can either repair the damage or move elsewhere. If this happens in the middle of winter and the animal is hibernating and wakes up, do the same, but bring out some food for a few nights to help it top up fat reserves. The complications start if there are babies. If there are, then replace the material, handling it as little as possible to reduce the amount of human scent you leave, and then retreat, but keep an eye on the nest to see if the mother returns. If there is no sign by the next morning, call a rescue centre (there is a list of numbers at the BHPS, either on the website or on the answerphone). Do be strict about restraining inquisitive friends. Everyone will want to see the babies I am sure, but the more they are disturbed, the greater chance they have of dying. And if the mother has returned, it is not unheard of for her to abandon or eat nestlings.

As you can see, there is a lot to think about when making your garden hedgehog-friendly, but much of it is common sense. And then this leaves you in a position to enjoy any hedgehogs that come your way, safe in the knowledge that you have done your best. So you can sit on the swing seat with a gin and tonic, happily watching the hedgehog show from beneath a warm blanket.

If that is not enough for you, there is some wonderful material available on how to rear abandoned baby hedgehogs; how to mimic the massaging lick of a mother hedgehog, stimulating her young to urinate and defecate; how to remove ticks from behind their ears; how to swab maggots from wounds and how to go about removing all further social engagements from your diary as you get sucked into a 24/7 world of hedgehog care. They can be found on the BHPS website, and you can also get in touch with the many hedgehog carers around the country, who will offer you advice. But beware. Hedgehogs can take over your life.

There is a superb description of how intense the relationship can be in *Dearest Prickles: The Story of a Hedgehog Family*, by Walter and Christl Poduschka. Published in 1972, this tells the tale of how the discovery of three baby hedgehogs in a garden changed their life. What is special about this is that they charted their progress meticulously, revealing the techniques that worked and not shying away from describing those that didn't. They discovered that there was nothing in the literature to direct them, so they used what skills they had to great effect.

I don't think that anyone would follow their advice on

feeding cow's milk any more, but the Poduschka story does prove it is not lethal. Sadly, the book is out of print, but it is to be recommended, especially for the description of the armpit fetish of one of the rescued animals. It would go wild over Walter's sweaty armpits and ended up gnawing a hole in his best shirt. I had a friend with a cat that would make a beeline for my armpit and just slip into ecstasy as it kneaded my side and mouthed my clothes. Do I smell like a lactating cat?

You might think it a trivial intervention to save a few baby hedgehogs, but they do not have life easy. Around a quarter die before leaving the nest and a half of the rest do not survive their first hibernation. In fact, it would not be unreasonable to suggest that hedgehogs are quite dependent on us for survival. After all, they are linked to the progress of humanity, though not in the most obvious of ways.

Someone is Eating the Suburban Doughnut – Doh!

Something quite unusual has happened in our relationship with hedgehogs, for we have affected their ability to thrive. Whiz back around 6,000 years and the UK was covered in the wildwood. Mesolithic foragers had cleared patches to assist in hunting. And those patches must have been very attractive to

 hedgehogs, providing, as they did, additional woodland edge habitat. But the arrival of Neolithic man was to see the beginning of the end of the primeval forests of this fair land. With their fancy agriculture, they began to make massive inroads into the seemingly infinite wildwood. And these new clearings provided even better habitat for hedgehogs.

Hedgehogs must have seen the coming of man as a great gift from an almighty spiny deity. No longer did they have to eke out a meagre existence surrounded by large trees, trying to find small clearings caused by fallen trees or lightning strikes. Suddenly they were presented with clearing after clearing as the wildwood retreated.

And imagine their delight at the coming of the Romans and then the Anglo-Saxons, both of whom used hedges as part of their agricultural systems. This is the sort of habitat that hedgehogs were made for and their numbers must have increased markedly. All the way until the arrival of the infernal combustion engine and the drive towards increased field size. Hedgehogs probably thought they were in paradise, give or take the little issue of misidentification as vermin, until the end of the Second World War and the beginning of modern agriculture.

As modernity imposed itself on the hedgehog's idyll and farmland was laid waste in the rush to produce more, the once biodiverse landscape of Britain was turning into a wildlife desert. So the doughty hedgehog needed to find a new home. And what better course of action than to follow all those nice tall bipeds, who were also being done out of a home in the countryside, into the new invention of suburbia.

Suburbia was perfect. Here was a rich and varied habitat.

Lawns – hedgehogs must have really thought the gods were smiling when they discovered lawns. Short legs mean wet tummies, but mown lawns means easy walking and no need to go grunting through undergrowth as worms pop up conveniently to the surface. And then those benevolent gardeners would sometimes put out food as well – and who cared if sometimes it was not quite what they would normally eat.

But now not all is well with suburbia and recently hedgehogs have come up against another challenge.

Picture, if you will, a doughnut. The urban centre is the empty bit in the middle and the surrounding countryside is the area beyond the sweet calorie-intense cake. And the cake itself is where the hedgehogs like best to be. But we are consuming the doughnut with alarming speed. Suburban gardens, the refuge of the hedgehog after they were driven from the countryside, are being lost to further development. Every back garden that becomes a block of flats, every front garden that becomes a car park, is a further nibble at the doughnut. This last point forced the usually oh so reasonable Jeremy Clarkson into making some rather unpleasant remarks. Writing in the *Sun*, he complained that if people are not allowed to pave their front gardens they will have to park further from their front door so that 'a disease-ridden rat with a punk hairdo can have somewhere to sleep'. I have to admit I quite enjoyed watching a friend custard-pie him when he visited Oxford.

There is also a worry that the tendency to create another room for the house out in the garden may be having an impact on the hedgehog. Patios and decking, complete with heaters, further remove hedgehog habitat from the garden. Perhaps the next logical step for the hedgehog is to accept dependence on humanity and throw themselves at our feet, begging for domestication. If we have made the outside so inhospitable that hedgehogs have nowhere left to thrive, all that is left for them is to take up residence on a wheel in a cage as a pet.

I hope that there is no dystopian future in which the only place left for the hedgehog is the pet shop.

The picture of our relationship with hedgehogs is complex. We are worried when it looks like we are losing them, yet in times past we have persecuted them with extreme prejudice. And when confronted with the tragic news of their decline, there can be a tendency to retreat into a ball of denial, hoping, while we hide away, that some experts will step forward to provide a solution. Well, there are some experts out there doing a fine job. But saving hedgehogs is not the preserve of experts. In fact, I believe the most important work will be done by you and me, by amateurs.

And this is not entirely altruistic. I believe that we are ignoring a very important point: hedgehogs can help us a great deal. We have already seen how individuals benefit enormously from immersing themselves in the world of hedgehogs. But I am sure that this benefit is not exclusively the preserve of hedgehog carers. There is a tendency to overestimate our understanding of the everyday and to underestimate its importance. There is much we can all gain from hedgehogs.

CHAPTER
EIGHT

*How Hedgehogs
Can Save
the World*

Some animals are charismatic. And of these a bunch known as the 'charismatic mega-fauna' get most of the attention. They are the poster children for international wildlife and environmental groups. Whether it is elephants, tigers or whales, these exquisite examples of evolution provide us with an opportunity to wonder at the beauty of the world. They can also be used as a warning. Do you love elephants? Well, people who trade in ivory are killing them, so you are killing them if you buy an ivory trinket on holiday.

And it works. Pandas may be an evolutionary dead end, doomed to extinction, but they are cute and they rake in the donations. Yet none of these animals are approachable. They may be charismatic, but they are distant, like supermodels. Yes, Kate Moss is aesthetically very pleasing, but there is no way I am going to get to know her. And if I did, do you think we would become friends? The same goes for elephants – beautiful, awe-inspiring, but very few people are going to get to know them. And they have some pretty bad habits too – hooligan teenagers destroying their home patch.

So, I would argue, we need to put these unobtainable beauties to one side and get realistic about our chances of finding true love. Because this is what we need. Love and compassion for nature are the best way to ensure we all, humans and animals, continue to survive on our one and only planet.

Remember, the only way you will get under the skin of a live tiger is if it eats you. And who needs tigers when it is possible to get under the skin of one of the most charismatic of creatures? An animal that is an icon for a country's wildlife; an animal so mundane that we barely give it a second thought until we notice it is gone; an animal that we can all have a chance of meeting. Like the girl or boy next door, the hedgehog is what true love is all about.

Getting moved and becoming passionate are key to us all becoming more involved in creating the change we want to see, and in fact becoming the change we want to see, to steal a line from Gandhi.

We can love a hedgehog like no other animal. It is the first and probably only wild animal that we urbanites and suburbanites have a chance of getting really close to. Feeding ducks doesn't count – you can throw bread at them, but have you ever felt any sort of bond? No. But the hedgehog chooses to share the same space as us and if we are willing to change our point of view and get down on its level, we will be rewarded by the opening of a door into a deeper understanding of the natural world. Once the connection has been made, once we have had that chance to do the nose-to-nose thing and see the spark of wild in its eye, then we can follow it through into a new world view.

There is a magical piece of music by Thomas Adès called 'Tevot' that surges from chaos to order, then order builds into love and love takes on an almost ethereal nature. And that is what hedgehogs can do for us. The world may be confusing, there may be a bewilderment of signals coming our way, but one strong theme can take us by the hand and lead us to a sanctuary, to something close to enlightenment: a true love of the world around us. Incidentally, 'Tevot' is Hebrew for 'ark', as in Noah's. Perhaps it will be the hedgehog that leads us aboard next time.

So we follow the hedgehog, if not up a ramp then at least its progress. We notice the dead on the road, but feel it a little more as we question the need for the journey that has dragged us into the car. We see the barrier that the road has become. Not the tarmac, actually quite attractive for a short legged beast, but the business that speeds along. We see the countryside change, fields expanding, hedges fading; we see suburbia change, gardens shrinking, traffic increasing. We are being gently guided to think a little bit more about the way we lead our lives. That is what is great in a new relationship: you get an opportunity to look at your own life through the eyes of your new significant other. We are most willing to change ourselves in the grip of true love.

True love, not the sort that tends to infect our appreciation of the natural world. I have run a workshop called 'Sentimentality: The Enemy of Ecology'. Sentimental love is superficial; it does not offer much. Bubblegum love. A sentimental affection can cause blindness to what is real. A sentimental reaction to the culling of hedgehogs on the Uists would be a simple refusal to accept it under any circumstances. If there had been clear evidence that a cull would have been more humane, then I would have had to support it.

That is not to say that sentimentality is without its uses. My love of nature began sentimentally – being attracted to the charismatic mega-fauna. I had a large poster of a tiger above my bed for many years. There was no way I could engage with a tiger. I wanted to work with animals, though, and have ended up allowing that sentimentality to lead me to something more profound. The risk with sentimentality is that it becomes a gluey swamp that binds in an unfulfilled state – and if we are not careful, the path out of the swamp is the one lit by the neon excess of consumerism.

Hedgehogs have more to teach us than an appreciation of the wild. A philosopher friend wondered if I had heard of Schopenhauer. Being more philistine than philosopher I admitted my ignorance and was introduced to the 'Hedgehog's Dilemma'. The idea is straightforward, if biologically not very accurate.

Two hedgehogs want to be together to share their love. However, the closer they get to each other, the more they hurt each other. They back away, but begin to feel lonely, so they move closer again until it hurts. And such is the dilemma: how can the hedgehogs be close enough together to share their love without causing pain?

Schopenhauer was not a biologist. If he had bothered to watch courting hedgehogs, he would have seen how they overcome the obvious obstacles to reproduction. I have mentioned the circling war of attrition already. When the time comes for the female to relent, she lets the male in by relaxing her spines and arching her back, with her head pointing up and her undercarriage slipping from beneath the skirt of spines. And while the male may have a prodigious penis (for his size), he is always aware that no means no. She can end the process with a frown.

Schopenhauer was interested in human relationships. How can someone get close enough to the one they love without causing pain, while at the same time not being so far away as to feel the pang of loneliness?

This got me thinking. What is the biggest, most all-encompassing relationship we have? I would argue that it is with the world around us. And I believe that humanity is suffering from the hedgehog's dilemma in this most vital of bonds.

We want to be close to the natural world – I would go so far as to say we need that contact. But if we get too close, we destroy it: we trample it; we take too much of the good out and dump too much of our bad in. And if we retreat from the natural world, into cities or industrialized agricultural landscapes, we become bereft, lonely. We become so disconnected from our roots that we easily forget the value of the natural world and accelerate its destruction.

The dilemma we face is in trying to get close enough to the wild without corrupting it out of existence.

The year 2008 is a big one for the planet. Not just because it marks the centenary of the identification of *hughi*, but because it is the year that the majority of humans will be living within urban environments for the first time. Removed from the natural world as never before, we have become an urban species. In just a few short generations we have gone from predominantly rural to mostly urban. And it was only a few moments earlier, on an evolutionary clock, that we were hunter-gatherers, eking out an existence as part of the natural world.

Is that separation anything to worry about? Should we be bothered by progress? Well, these arguments always sell better if you make it black and white. But I am an ecologist and I know that life is never so simple.

Progress is great. Separation from the elements and from the diseases and predators in the natural world is wonderful and I love my iPod. But too little connection with the wild is not a good thing. The hedgehog's dilemma is not just theoretical. We lose something very important. All those hundreds of thousands of years as hunter-gatherers have left their mark inside each and every one of us. There was a set of environmental criteria that improved the chances of our prehistoric self surviving and they are somehow ingrained in our DNA. Like the tern, with its migration route map, we cannot point to the 'gene for', but there is something hard-wired into our make-up: 'biophilia'.

Edward Wilson, who developed this idea, defines biophilia as 'the innately emotional affiliation of human beings to other living organisms. Innate means hereditary and hence part of ultimate human nature.' He describes how we have a dependency on the natural world in excess of our basic physical needs; that it extends to our aesthetic, intellectual and emotional needs as well.

This is an idea that has been picked up by many important thinkers and writers, such as Richard Mabey. His beautiful book, *Nature Cure*, charts his emergence from a painful depression, drawn out of his slough thanks to an active, sensual re-engagement with nature.

And can't we all feel that gladdening of the heart when we find ourselves embraced by nature? I know that I will feel better if I get out of the city and immerse myself in a bit of wild. It does not have to be much, but I know it works and I know I am not alone. A report published in 2007 for the RSPB called *Natural Thinking* presented evidence that contact with nature and green space has a very positive effect on our mental health. And American author Richard Louv has taken Wilson's idea further, identifying 'nature-deficit disorder' as a condition that afflicts our modern selves. I can really appreciate that phrase – it makes utter sense. I can feel the tension in my shoulders and behind my eyes ease as effectively as a deep-tissue massage when I climb the hill that looks over a beach in Gower, South Wales, and just allow the wind and the sky to knead me back into shape.

There have been very real benefits noted from this sort of 'green cure'. Research shows that if you measure the recovery of people in a hospital – people receiving the same care for the same illness – the ones with a view of a brick wall get better more slowly than the ones with a view of trees or parkland. And there is plenty of evidence that the most sustainable response to depression is not drugs but exercise in a natural landscape.

Strangely, it seems that Feng Shui cottoned on to this earlier, much earlier. At least in some examples of this ancient art of furniture placement, there is a strong resonance with the natural world. Ignore the astrological bunkum and consider that the perfect Feng Shui home is situated on a slope, overlooking water in a rural scene. This is just like the perfect retreat for hunter-gatherers on the plains of east Africa, where humanity evolved. A slope would provide a view over savannah, a view towards the water where wildlife would congregate, a view that would present opportunities to see predators and prey.

I am sure it is no coincidence that Capability Brown's trademark landscapes, such as the gardens surrounding Blenheim Palace in Oxfordshire, mimic this feel as well.

Hedgehogs provide us with a way out of their dilemma. We cannot all live in a perfectly biophilic home – places like Blenheim are rare and unsurprisingly exclusive. But there is a way we can gain something of that contact with nature; meet some of those needs that lurk deep in our genes. The way is obvious: hedgehogs. They give us the opportunity to get close to the natural world. But this only works as long as we remain conscious of the impact we have on our guides. Hedgehogs can do more to foment change in our attitudes towards the environment than almost any other animal. It is only a short walk from thinking of the hedgehog as a rather cute garden visitor to realizing that the roads you drive on to the supermarket or the holidays you take all have an impact on your new-found friend. Busy roads bisect the land, fragmenting hedgehog habitat. Supermarkets demand centralized food production, which only becomes economic on a massive scale, with larger machines working larger fields, fields bereft of hedges. Hedgehogs are like spiny canaries, warning us of the explosive mix in the atmosphere.

The journey hedgehogs have led me on has taken me from a sentimental love of wildlife through a pragmatic desire to understand more and into something quite special. But there is no way I am unique in this. There is a gateway here to be stepped through by every one of us – just follow the busy little hedgehog, like Lucie did.

Lucie enters the world of the hedgehog and finds it warm, safe and industrious. We too can follow her lead, and if we catch a glimpse of something on a hillside, or hear a snuffle in our garden, why not take a chance? You might meet your very own Mrs Tiggy-Winkle. And while she will not be wearing an apron (though don't get me started on the American pet hedgehogs, all dressed up in dolls' clothes) and will, probably, not talk, I reckon we would all do well to stop and listen. So much can be said without words, so don't be shy, get down on your hands and knees, lean forward and see what happens as you get nose to nose with a hedgehog. Relish and wallow in the moment of making a connection with the most charismatic creature on the planet. Look into those wild hedgehog eyes and, if you are lucky, catch a glimpse of a special something, a spark that can change your entire life.

Hedgehog-friendly Organizations

If you find a sick or injured hedgehog, and you want to help, the best bet is to get in touch with one of the many experts around the country. There is a county by county list on the British Hedgehog Preservation Society's website – and also details of regional contacts on their answerphone.

British Hedgehog Preservation Society
Hedgehog House, Dhuston, Ludlow, Shropshire SY8 3PL
01584 890801
www.britishhedgehogs.org.uk

The BHPS website also has a host of other useful information about ways you can improve the lot of hedgehogs in your area – and even a guide to how to care for a sick hedgehog if you are brave enough to go down that path.

People who have gone down that path are Gay and Andy Christie from Hessilhead. They are not set up for visitors, but they do have an open day each year. So if you are in the area at the right time, it is well worth a visit – a truly inspirational place. And you can get an indication of the amount of work they do by having a look at Gay's diary on their website.

Hessilhead Wildlife Rescue Trust, Gateside, Beith, Scotland
KA15 1HT
01505 502415
www.hessilheadwildlife.org.uk

Les Stocker's Tiggywinkles empire is open to the public and well worth a visit – and do not forget the hedgehog museum either. Details of how to get there are on the website, or give them a call.

Tiggywinkles, The Wildlife Hospital Trust, Aston Road, Haddenham, Aylesbury, Buckinghamshire HP17 8AF UK
01844 292292
www.sttiggywinkles.org.uk

Caroline Gould at Vale gives a clear indication of just what goes into running such a centre with her blog.

Vale Wildlife Rescue, Station Road, Beckford, Tewkesbury, Gloucestershire GL20 7AN
01386 882288
www.vwr.org.uk

But there is much more to hedgehogs than just patching them up. One of the best points of contact for conservation and research about hedgehogs is the People's Trust for Endangered Species – and the associated Mammals Trust. These are the people, along with scientists like Pat Morris, who are looking into the problems hedgehogs face and trying to identify solutions.

People's Trust for Endangered Species and the Mammals Trust, 15 Cloisters House, 8 Battersea Park Road, London SW8 4BG
020 7498 4533
www.ptes.org

And if you were intrigued at the idea of hedgehog pet keeping, then the IHA is a good place to start looking for more information. Run in part by Standing Bear, it can link you through to discussion forums where you can have a look at the sorts of issues confronting pet keepers, and will hopefully put you off trying to get started with pet hedgehogs in the UK.

International Hedgehog Association
www.hedgehogclub.com